Standing the Test of Time

The Autobiography of Bill Alley
(as told to Pat Symes)

Manchester
EMPIRE PUBLICATIONS

First published in 1999

EMPIRE PUBLICATIONS LTD
62 Charles Street, Manchester M1 7DF

© Bill Alley 1999

ISBN 1-901746-06-2

Typeset by
Michael Hubbard
and printed in Great Britain
by MFP Design & Print
Longford Trading Estate
Thomas Street
Stretford
Manchester M32 0JT

Contents

List of Illustrations

ACKNOWLEDGEMENTS

Most of what you are about to read in this book was first written in 1984, when I had just retired from the First Class Umpires' list. To my amazement, the powers that be at the T.C.C.B. at the time decided that what I had written was too controversial and that I had over-stepped the mark! Consequently, the book was laid to rest and only recently given a new breath of life, for which I am truly grateful as it also coincides with my 80th birthday and my 50th wedding anniversary.

For this I would like to give thanks to Pat Symes, who had the stamina and perseverance to transcribe many hours of interviews, firstly in 1984 and then again more recently to update and refine the content. I would also like to thank Jim Baldwin for checking the many facts in the book. I have played, umpired and watched a lot of cricket in my lifetime, so inevitably some events, dates and teams became confused and it is thanks to Jim that they have been corrected. On the same theme, I would like to thank Andy Searle of Empire Publications, who had no hesitation in reviving the project and saw it through from manuscript to publication. Thanks, too, to my old sparring partner Tom Graveney, one of the greatest batsmen I ever played against, for providing the foreword.

I would especially like to thank my wife Betty, who has been my constant companion and inspiration for 50 years, never grumbling and always supportive of everything I have ever done. No man could have wished for a better partner in life. To the people of Somerset, where I have lived for the last 42 years, I also extend a massive hand of thanks. In my opinion, it is the most beautiful part of England and Betty and I have been so happy living here.

Lastly, I would like to thank all cricketers and umpires that I have played with or met anywhere in the world. Cricket is the best game in the world and has given me more pleasure than I can ever have dreamt of when I first took up the game all those years ago. To cricket people everywhere, thanks for the memory.

Just one last comment. When I originally wrote this book I deplored the lack of leg-spin bowling in world cricket and forecast that after Abdul Qadir we may never see their like again. I am happy to admit that I made a mistake in that department. It gladdened my heart to see, in the recent Ashes contest in Australia, two leg-spinners operating at the same time – and winning a Test match – for my native country in Sydney, the ground where I started my First Class cricket career. Just maybe things are not as bad in modern cricket as oldies like myself try to make out!

Bill Alley
Taunton
3rd February, 1999

FOREWORD

by Tom Graveney O.B.E.

What a pleasure to write a few words about my old friend Bill Alley - if the book is like the man it should be a best seller. I first met Bill when he was playing league cricket in Blackpool in the early fifties. Gloucestershire were playing Lancashire at Stanley Park and naturally we had a few beers after the game. Almost immediately he found Somerset and since then he was one of the men I looked forward to playing with and against.

He was a tremendous cricketer who never gave anything but 100%- except once! We were touring Pakistan with an International XI raised by Alf Gover and captained by Peter Richardson - we had half the West Indian side and were a very powerful outfit. The unofficial Test at Lahore was played on a beautiful pitch and everyone scored runs. When Pakistan batted Charlie Griffith and Chester Watson failed to break the opening stand and Bill came on second change. One four came off his first over, two off the second and second ball of his third over he pulled up in agony - I'll never bowl again! I seem to recall the next season when we, Worcestershire, were playing at the Imperial Ground in Bristol he bowled 43 overs on the trot because of injuries to Fred Rumsey and Ken Palmer!

After our retirement the Whitbread Wanderers were formed - mainly Worcestershire and Gloucestershire ex-players, plus Bill and Neil Hawke from Australia, and others, so we carried on enjoying our cricket for a few years more. Even now, when I visit Taunton, I can usually find Bill somewhere on the ground and we always talk over the great times we had - particularly when sharing a room for seven weeks in Pakistan. Bill was one of those special cricketers - a great international both on and off the field.

1
The Boy from Brooklyn

THE TOWN OF BROOKLYN is unlikely ever to be famous. It lies either side of the main railway line between Sydney and Newcastle on the Hawkesbury River, relies heavily on oyster fishing for its income, and was the early home of one William Edward Alley.

I was born in the nearby town of Hornsby, New South Wales on 3rd February 1919 only because Brooklyn was not big enough to have a hospital of its own. My father worked in the Government service as a warder and I was the eldest of his six children. We lived with my grandmother while I was a youngster, and when my parents moved two miles to a home of their own, she gave them an ultimatum: "If you go, he stops with me."

That's how I came to be brought up by my grandmother in what I realise now was a poor community in which I was one of the more privileged children. My Grandmother tended to spoil me a little and I was one of only three out of about 90 at school who had the luxury of a pair of shoes. Not that any of the other children were in any way jealous, because being bare-footed was normal and I was the odd one out. I remember how often these children used to cut open their feet and, I am afraid, medical treatment was crude and basic in those days. Any wound was wrapped in a mixture of bandage and kerosene and stitches were a novelty.

We expected nothing else from a little town of 2,000 people 36 miles from Sydney, 15 miles from the nearest dentist, with no resident doctor and only one pub in which to kill any pain. Electricity was for the rich – so was television, and in my grandmother's house it was bed by candlelight. It was a tough place to be brought up in but it stood me in good stead later in life and I don't think I was ever unhappy. My grandmother kept me busy, kicking me out of bed at dawn to chop wood and feed the chickens. Only then could

1

Standing the Test of Time

I go on to school or out into the streets to play cricket with the other youngsters.

It will come as a surprise to many admirers that I was no great shakes at school. To be honest, I was useless at anything other than simple reading and writing and, if I possibly could, I got out of it. The only interest I had was the school garden and my diligence and effort amongst the shrubs was rewarded when I received a prize for best gardener. I suppose the teachers gave it to me as some sort of compensation because I was certainly never going to pick up anything for a more academic subject. We had a teacher in these days by the name of Newman, who was obliged to take his own infant into class. He was a violent tempered man (I suppose he had to be with pupils like me) and it was not uncommon to see him standing at the front of the class with his child under one arm and waving a cane furiously with the other.

Apart from the floral splendour of Alley's gardens, the only relief came from sport and, in particular, cricket. Cricket was the street game. We all played it like they do soccer in England and baseball in America and I soon discovered that I was good at it. Every lunchtime I would run home the best part of three miles to my grandmother's house for some food and then run back again just to play the game in the schoolyard before the bell summoned us to our desks again.

My ability at cricket more than made up for my struggles in the classroom. Even from an early age, I had a good eye for the ball and an equally good pair of hands. Year after year I won awards for the best batsman and best bowler and a little cup for the most catches. I may not have been up to much at anything else, but when it came to cricket I was the hero of most of the town.

Cricket, of course, became my life for the best part of 40 years, during which I travelled the world and played at all the major venues, but in those days it was a relaxation; a game to be enjoyed and any thought of making a living out of it was pure fantasy. Bradman was the big name at the time, but there was no chance of seeing him in action and places like Lord's, the Oval or even the Melbourne

Cricket Ground might just as well have been on the moon. Any lingering ambition to play the game I loved for a living disappeared for ever, I thought, when Brooklyn school said good riddance and turned me out on to the world at the age of 14 and, like many of my mates, I headed inevitably for the oyster farms.

As a youngster, my one glimpse of the sort of living top class cricketers could enjoy came when my grandmother, sensing I was good at something, bought me a cricket bat and took me on the train to Sydney to get it signed by the great Bradman. Imagine our shock when we reached there. In front of us was a queue stretching for what seemed like a mile, all of them pleading for his autograph and a kind word from the nation's hero. As Bradman dispensed his favours, we stood in the heat for the best part of three hours as the queue got smaller – and then came a bigger shock. For the honour of signing my new bat Bradman demanded seven shillings and sixpence, a lot of money in those days. I was stunned, but after standing in a queue for that length of time there was no way I was going home without getting that signature. Looking back on it, Sir Don must have made a tidy sum that day, and I don't blame him one little bit. You can forget Packer and what has happened since in cricket because, in my opinion, Bradman was the first man to realise the commercial potential of the game – and to exploit it.

Seven shillings and sixpence was the size of my first week's pay packet from the oyster fisheries. My grandmother snatched it as I came through the door and gave me a shilling of it back to spend as I saw fit. It was a hard job but enjoyable and in those days I never had any expectations that I might do anything else in life, and certainly not play cricket.

My view of the outside world came from the occasional visit to a cinema. Tom Mix was my hero and I knew all the film stars as if they were personal friends. Otherwise, apart from numerous dawn-till-dusk games of street cricket, my mates and I would wander into the outback, walking up to 20 miles looking for wild beehives and never squealing when we got stung – as we always did. As a special diversion we organised twenty-mile paper chases in the countryside around Brooklyn, racing past startled wallabies along the route. It was simple, honest fun and the limit of our small world.

Sydney was not the city of gleaming skyscrapers it is today when, as raw and impressionable country boys, my great friend Ian Cross, and I used to get on the first train and head towards its mass of red corrugated roofed houses. Our routine never varied. As soon as the train pulled into Central Station, we dived into the nearest pub in George or Pitt streets. This was followed by a meal of the biggest meat pies we ever set eyes on and then on to a movie. It was back into the pub after the films were over and an unsteady path back to the station for the last train home. It took me weeks to save up for a meal like that, but man did I enjoy them!

It was wartime and Sydney was filled with British and American troops on their way to the world's trouble spots. A ship laden with troops provided a big event in the lives of those of us who had been in Australia ever since we had first seen the light of day. And I can tell you we were not pleased to see them. The Poms got stuck in to the drink but the Americans had money, plenty of it. They snapped up all the local women and it was nearly impossible to get a taxi. The Sydney taxi-drivers pulled away from the curbside when they realised you did not have an American accent. They used to double their charges and the Americans never complained. I had a bit of a reputation as a fighter in those days, but I can assure you I was not among the gangs of Sydney-siders who went out looking for and beating up the Yanks. Mind you, I didn't try to stop them.

These Americans were big men and as a teenager I was very small, no more than 5 ft 4 ins until I suddenly shot up soon after I received a handy piece of advice from a Sydney cricketer by the name of Vic Trumper, the son of the great cricketer of the same name. As a tiny batsman in club cricket I was at a real disadvantage against short-pitched bowling, so Vic took me aside and came up with a remedy for my lack of inches. "Bill" he said. "There is one sure-fire solution. Whenever you can, go and stand in a cow dung." I was only a lad and desperate to grow and I'll admit now to putting one foot in a cow pat when I thought no one was looking. Much to

4

my surprise, I leapt up to well over six feet soon after Vic had delivered his homespun theory. Perhaps he knew something the rest of us did not.

My lack of inches did not stop me from becoming something of a star-turn in Brooklyn club cricket. When I was 15 and 16 I was scoring runs at a ferocious rate, averaging 90, and in one incredible season rattled up eleven centuries. This provided me with a bonus I had not anticipated and gave me my first taste of the sweet pickings of sponsorship. A Sports outfitters in Hornsby promised me a pair of their best shoes for every century I scored while wearing some of their cricket boots. The match umpires had to sign a form indicating I had indeed scored the runs while kitted out in the boots which carried the shop's label. I will let you into a secret now. The boots belonged to another shop but I switched the labels to fool the umpires and to collect my prize. That year I won eleven pairs of shoes – and I sold the lot.

At Brooklyn we played on a concrete and matting wicket and the standard of the opposition was by no means brilliant. Our nearest rivals were 15 miles away and before every home match the local publican delivered an 18-gallon keg of beer to help quench the thirst of the players of both sides. It was an honourable gesture but it often backfired. The matches were scheduled to start at 10.30 and it wasn't uncommon for some of the players to have a little taster before they took to the field. By lunchtime some of the lads were showing more interest in the beer than they were in the cricket and by teatime some players had a job to stand. I remember many a time when beer-induced arguments began and then fights broke out all over the place. Before long, people were piling in from all directions and toppling into the River Hawkesbury on the end of many a furious straight left. We took our cricket seriously, but in some cases the drinking took priority.

Still, the rustic nature of the cricket did not stop me building some huge scores and winning a 12 inch high cup for taking 67 catches in a season at first slip. I suppose it was obvious to me that at that age I had ability well above the average, but it never occurred to me that I might make any kind of life from the game, despite my early dip into sponsorship. I was very much the big fish on the end of the Hawkesbury River and, while I was amassing centuries and collecting cups, I was quite content to carry on that way.

I think a more likely reason for my sudden growth was the hard physical work I had to endure when I left the tranquil peace of the oyster farms to work as a machinist, drilling a tunnel in the dark, coughing up dust and grafting like I have never grafted since. I can't say I enjoyed it but, looking back, it must have done me some good. When I finally emerged into the daylight, my job done years later, I was a strong and sturdy six-footer, weighing-in at about 11 stone 10 lbs. and powerful with it. The war was on and I wanted to join the army like some of my friends, but the job I was doing was considered too valuable to the government, working my way through the tunnel by the Hawkesbury, and I was given four exemptions from military service. All the while my poor grandmother was running a guesthouse and struggling to keep me in clothes as I grew by the day.

Cricket was the big inspiration of my life as I grew up in Brooklyn, but I took up boxing and was immediately successful. I had 28 fights and won the lot, and there was even talk once that I was close to a shot at the world welterweight title, but I can assure you I was a very long way from any such thing. They were as much brawls as fights and I took some terrible pastings even as the winner. I used to stare in the mirror the next morning surveying the damage and wondering what on earth my opponent must be looking like. Even so, I took it all seriously enough and was still boxing for a few bob a time by the time I graduated to the New South Wales state side. It was an accident – bizarre in retrospect – in the nets at Adelaide which put paid to my boxing career and almost put an end to Bill Alley.

The New South Wales team were in the nets getting in some practice at Adelaide before the start of a Shield match against South Australia. I was bending down to pick up a ball as Jock Livingston in an adjoining net played a hook shot. The ball went through a weak section of the net and crashed into the left side of my jaw. I was knocked out instantly and for two and a half days battled for my life in hospital in a coma. Team-mates were certain I was never going to pull through after such a fearful blow. Doctors could not even operate until I came round, and then came the job of piecing together my shattered jaw.

I had 60 stitches in the wound and surgeons told me that a couple of inches higher and I would have been killed. I was a lucky man and luckier still that the injury has left me no lasting damage to my face. Not surprisingly, a specialist told me to forget about boxing. Another blow in the same place might finish me off. I took his advice and my boxing career, such as it was, came to an end.

At the end of the war I was told there was plenty of work in Sydney for a skilled labourer like me so I headed for the big city, making a living in all kinds of jobs where a brawny bloke was best suited. I was a blacksmith's striker, a boilermaker's helper and a mail cartrimmer's assistant, using the muscles which were one day going to stand me in such good stead on the cricket pitch. Of course, it was hard work but I was a strong lad and in any case there was not much in the way of alternatives for someone with no academic qualifications of any kind. By way of little light relief, and to earn myself some extra cash, my cricketing pal Ken Grieves – later to play for New South Wales and Lancashire – fixed me up with a job as his replacement as a bouncer on the door of a Sydney ballroom. He said, "Bill, you'll have no trouble here. The customers are as good as gold." I made the mistake of believing him. On my first night alone, I got involved in three big fights and a smaller one.

There was one man, a ginger-haired Scotsman, who with a few drinks in his belly was ready to take on anyone. And that usually meant me. Every week for nine weeks we did battle on the ballroom stairs. No matter how hard I hit him – and remember, I could handle myself in the boxing ring – he got up and gave as good as he got. After every scrap, and with blood streaming down his face, he would say to me, "I'll see you next week." Four or five years later when I returned to Australia on a visit from England, I made a sentimental journey to that ballroom and I could hardly believe my eyes when I climbed the steps. Guarding the door as if his life depended on it was that self-same wildman from Scotland. "Do you want to finish it now" he said. For a moment I thought he meant it. He was the bouncer now. But we finally shook hands and went inside for a drink; friends at last.

All of this might give the impression I was too busy to have any time to take cricket seriously, but one day I received an invitation for a little trial at Waitower Oval at Hornsby. If I was good enough there was the chance to play for Northern Districts in the Sydney Grade competition, a big step up from the sort of cricket I was used to with Brooklyn. I did as well as could be expected in the trial and before long I was making runs in the in Northern Districts' first team. I had always wanted to play at Hornsby. The ground was the best for miles around and the facilities far better than anything I had ever previously experienced. If I had an ambition in cricket it was to play at Waitower. Once this was achieved I felt I had made the big-time and for four or five years I pitted my skills against the best in the city in the sure knowledge this was as high as I was ever going to go.

When I first arrived at Hornsby I had plenty to live up to. I was the great hope of Brooklyn and carried all their ambitions with me. As a batsman I was soon among the runs, quickly adjusting to the better class of bowling and before long breaking all club records with the same ease I broke them at Brooklyn. As a bowler my leg spinning days were soon brought to halt forever. Frankie Gilmor, the New South Wales fast bowler, broke down with injury and being big I was asked to fill the gap with some hastily contrived medium pace stuff. It worked a treat. I was soon among the wickets and, since I now knew I had two strings to my bow, my batting flourished.

Being able to bat and bowl medium pace I was always guaranteed work during the rest of my playing career in the Lancashire League, on tour with representative sides and with Somerset, but I do regret not being able to continue as a leg spinner because it is an art form which sadly almost came close to extinction.

The Boy from Brooklyn

It is comparatively simple to bowl a mean length and line with a bit of negative seam bowling, as I admit I did in 30 odd years of playing. It is a different matter trying to outwit batsmen with flight and spin. I suppose I should not grumble because I picked up 768 wickets in first class cricket and many more at lower levels with the style thrust upon me in that emergency, but I often wonder how many I might have got if I had been allowed to persevere with my back-of-the-hand deliveries.

After completing a further 16 years on the list of first class umpires in England in 1984, I could say with all honesty that a top class leg spinner could have been as much in demand and be just as successful as any of that awesome battery of West Indian fast bowling. I wonder how many other leg spinners who, like me, were persuaded to turn to something less frail and more economical and, over the years, have had cause to look back and regret what might have been.

I think I can say without conceit that I soon became the big star of Northern Districts, and for the first time I began to think in terms of playing for the state side and with it the chance to take on as an equal some of the great players of post-war cricket. For some reason I was ignored by the New South Wales team, and by the time I reached my middle twenties I was convinced my chance had slipped by. A curious twist in my life opened up the belated opportunity of playing for my state.

I married a Brooklyn girl named Irene after two years of courtship. Her aunt lived in the Petersham area of Sydney and we decided to move there because of the chance of some accommodation. It was the natural thing to do, to leave Northern Districts where I had set up a batting record in 1942-43 of 1,026 runs and join Petersham, where Grieves and Dudley Seddon provided a powerful backbone to the team. I am pleased to say it was a turning point in my career and I never looked back.

I had soon gathered a reputation for big hitting and I continued to play this way when I moved to Petersham. Cricket was a hobby reserved for a Saturday afternoon and, in my estimation, there was no better way of winding down from a hard week's work than by winding up to hit as many sixes and fours as possible. In truth I did not have much of a defence and it could be that the state selectors had written me off as a crude slogger. But I started to score runs at a rate and in such quantities that they could no longer ignore my claims. Against Randwick I plundered 265 in one afternoon, with 12 sixes and 24 fours, and later the same day finished off our opponents with 8 for 27. Faced with that sort of achievement my selection was only a matter of time.

For two seasons in succession I topped 1,000 runs, and in one memorable summer clocked up 1,254 runs, a grade aggregate which has not yet been beaten. Funnily enough, Geoff Boycott of all people came close to toppling it when he spent a season with Waverley 30 or so years later. Geoff likes beating batting records and by all accounts he was after mine. The following English summer he was back in the Test side and it was during the match at Headingly against the Australians while he was clocking up his 100th century in a match England won by an innings that we had a little chat. Geoff was at my end, the non-striker's, when he turned to me in a lull in play and said: "I suppose you want to know why I didn't beat your record?" Before I had time to answer, a single took him down the other end for a few minutes. Later we were reunited. Just as he was turning to tell me, I chipped in first. "I'll tell you why," I said. "Because you're not bloody good enough."

At the start of the 1945 season, at the advanced age of 26, the state selectors at least felt obliged to take a look at me and they could hardly have chosen a worse match for me than a clash with Marrickville on a nasty wicket and against Ernie Toshack, the left-armer who went on to play for Australia. I remember the pitch was flooded overnight and failure that day would almost certainly have consigned me to grade cricket forever. I had to make a big score – and I did.

2
Tragedy

I FELT LIKE A KING playing for New South Wales, but it could have left me like a pauper because it was an expensive privilege playing first-class cricket in Australia in those days. It was a great honour to have someone else pay your rail fare to other state capitals I had never before visited and to put you up in the best hotels. For a self-taught cricketer like me the chance to play in Melbourne, Brisbane and Adelaide on some of the finest tracks in the world, and in front of big crowds, was a tremendous bonus, particularly in my case because I was getting on a bit at 26 when it all started happening. I had to pinch myself at times when I played at the SCG to think of the great names who had been afforded the same wonderful opportunities in the past. Everyone who reached state level was instantly in the public eye, and for an up-country boy like me it was all too much. From the concrete and matting of Brooklyn to the SCG was a huge step, and now that my chance had come I was determined to take it.

Bradman may have moved on to South Australia but the New South Wales side immediately after the war was a strong one, some said so strong it could have held its own at international level. Ray Lindwall – the great Lindwall – was in his prime. Sid Barnes, Arthur Morris and Bill O'Reilly were also in the line-up when I made my debut fresh from grade cricket and at this level a raw novice; a cricketing midget among giants. We had so many good players from which to choose a team that fringe candidates with ambitions to play representative cricket were obliged to move to the weaker states like Queensland and, with due respect to Bradman, South Australia. Victoria were the old enemy and had the players to match us, like the magnificent all-rounder Keith Miller, Bill Johnston and Ian Johnson. Games against them at the Melbourne Cricket Ground and at Sydney were great occasions, the equivalent of a Liverpool-Everton football match – and taken just as seriously.

As a man I have never been short of confidence in my own ability, but it needed a strong nerve to look these sort of guys in the eye and say, "I'm as good as you, mate". I decided to stick to my old philosophy – to attack from the first ball and to take the consequences. I might have been forgiven for adopting a more cautious approach having taken so long to reach the top, but it was not the way I played cricket and there was no way I was going to alter now.

My early days with New South Wales saw me opening the innings and bowling my medium pace third change – and I lapped it up. My aggressive style could have got me into trouble at the top of the innings but I was instantly successful, just as I had been at Brooklyn, Northern Districts and Petersham. In my first season, 1945-6, I scored 485 runs at an average of 69.28 from seven matches. More importantly, I bridged the gap with three centuries, against South Australia in Adelaide and Sydney and another against the powerful Australian Services in Sydney.

I often think I might have been a better player had I been more defensive, but if I needed convincing my aggressive policy was the best one then my first season with New South Wales answered any personal questions. For the rest of my career I retained this attitude; if the ball is there to be hit, for Christ's sake, hit it. When I was an umpire I used to see big, strong lads scratching around for a few runs here and there and I would think to myself: "What are they scared of?" But then, I had never been coached in my life and I really only ever knew how to play one way – my way.

One of the aspects of life at the top which disappointed me was the state of the wickets in those days in Australia. They were never covered and, on some occasions, were decidedly sticky, particularly if I was forced to open the innings. But my biggest grouse was the finance. It cost me money for the privilege of playing with all these outstanding performers. We were paid 25 shillings per day and made to feel we were lucky to be getting anything. This would have been quite acceptable had I not been losing my wages at the same time. I was forced to take unpaid holiday whenever I got the call to play. For other, more illustrious, players in comfortable, sponsored jobs it was no hardship. For me, a humble labourer, it was a problem with which I could not readily come to terms.

I was never in a position to complain about the poor rewards but, when I hear of the big money now being poured into the game, I realise how fortunate modern players are and I often wonder what they would have made of the sort of cash being offered when I was in my prime.

Arthur Morris replaced me as opener and I moved down the order to number four, one place behind Barnes, who was the one man always to beat me in the averages. Barnes was a character and his clashes with Miller were always spiced with a certain edge. In my view Miller is the greatest all-rounder since the war, slightly better than Sobers, but more of that later. Miller was a tremendous competitor and an exceptional cricketer in all departments. He could go out drinking and womanising at night and maybe not return until gone day-break, but he never gave less than 100% once play was called early next morning.

Barnes and I figured in a big stand when he was performing against us for the Australian Services. Barnes and Miller struck a bet for five pounds before play began. Barnes told Miller he was going to get a hundred against him, one for each pound. Now Miller was a betting man and he was shaking hands on it before the offer had left Sid's lips. I would never have bet against Miller in any circumstances and, remember, £100 was a colossal amount of money in those days. As I remember it, Miller came in with tremendous speed and ferocity at Barnes and let him have his full repertoire. Sid had not even got off the mark when he edged Miller to first slip where Lindsay Hassett put down the catch. Miller let forth a stream of curses; Sid smiled weakly, like a man reprieved from the gallows, got his head down and scored his century. By nightfall, Keith Miller was £100 poorer.

My form in that first season not only secured my place in the state side, but started the papers talking about me as a possible Test player. I was flattered in spite of the ease with which I settled in because – and this is not false modesty – I had simply never looked upon myself as a potential international player. As I saw it, I was slightly above average in an era of great Australian players, but far too risky in my approach to be taken seriously at the highest level. I considered myself lucky to be playing for New South Wales and anything else was a complete dream.

Don Bradman came to watch me perform in one state match and shook me rigid when he called me aside. "Bill", he said, "You only have to stay fit to be on the boat to New Zealand for the tour". Coming from the mouth of the great man himself, I took it as official confirmation and approval. For the next few days I was walking on air. Just a matter of months previously I was a club cricketer, rolling up for a bit of relaxation, sometimes straight off the night shift. Now I was heading for an all-expenses paid Test tour on the nod from Bradman himself. My heart skipped a beat when I thought of the players the Australians would be taking on that tour – and I was to be one of them. Sid Barnes would be going, so too Hassett, Lindwall, Ian Johnson, Bill O'Reilly, Bruce Dooland of South Australia, Bill Brown, the Queensland player, and my old sparring partner, Ernie Toshack. It was difficult to imagine myself being considered in the same class, but in fairness to myself I had been outstanding in my first season and there was no reason why I should not have been in the selectors' minds.

On the strength of Bradman's encouragement I literally packed my bags and I went into town and bought myself twelve very expensive shirts in readiness for the tour. I suppose I was taking everything for granted, but my mind was racing on even beyond New Zealand. An England tour was looming in 1948 and it is the ambition of every Australian to earn the chance to take on the Poms. On the night before the team for New Zealand was due to be announced I could hardly sleep and the following day went slowly, as slowly as I can ever remember a day passing. Can you imagine my feelings then when I passed a newspaper stand to see the placards exclaim "Alley Tragedy"? I was absolutely numbed when I bought a paper and looked hastily through the names of the tour party. W.E. Alley was not among them. I was staggered, shell-shocked, call it what you will. Ronnie Hamence of South Australia was evidently preferred to me and it was hard to take. Ronnie never achieved averages to compare with mine, and I don't think he was successful either in New Zealand or in England two years later. I often think that had I been chosen instead of him, I too might have looked forward with confidence to a trip to England with Bradman's Aussies. Such is fate. As for the headlines, many people thought I had died or taken my own life, but as far as I was concerned a tragedy it was.

Just to compound my misery and gloom, Ernie Toshack came around to my house when I was out one day and, after introducing himself to my wife, pointed out that he had heard how I had purchased twelve white shirts and now that I would not be needing them she might just as well let him have them. Talk about adding insult to injury! When I came back my shirts had gone and so had my hopes of playing for my country.

My first season with New South Wales was far and away my best. In the next two years I played only five times for the state side, with injuries taking their toll and preventing me from consolidating spectacular first impressions. In 1946-7 I played only twice, with a top score of 43 not out made against Wally Hammond's MCC tourists. Cartilage trouble limited my movement and it dogged me for the next two years. Then came my fearful accident in the Adelaide nets and a broken finger, sustained in another match, completed an unhappy period. In my third year I played only three times and averaged a mere 11.20 with the bat, but I felt even at 29 years old that if I could put the injuries behind me there was still plenty of cricket in me and a place to England was by no means out of the question.

Certainly the disappointment of that time did not put off the Lancashire League clubs. In those days clubs in the north of England had a network of scouts in Australia, all of whom were paid handsomely for inducing top class young Aussies to go over and seek their fortunes. When I told you how little we were paid for playing for our state side it is little wonder that fat contracts from league clubs were greedily snapped up. The Australian Board of Control and the individual states were not happy to see the best young talent being drained in such a way but were apparently powerless to do anything about it – or reluctant to do so. They regarded a young man accepting a league offer in the same way the average Briton would regard a political defector to the Russians. But it was their fault for not attempting to keep us at home. After all, if you have a talent which inevitably disappears with time, then you should use it, and as a big-hitting batsman who could bowl at medium pace I was just the sort of player league clubs would have sold the local town hall for and I was greatly in demand. Leicestershire had a couple of Australians playing for them and they made me an offer, but it paled in comparison with the sort of money being talked about by the clubs in the Lancashire League. I rejected Leicestershire's offer without too much consideration, partly because of the problems of moving 12,000 miles and partly because the league offers were so much better.

Rawtenstall made me an offer I felt bound to accept and I had no hesitation in accepting their terms, but at the last minute it was all called off because one of the conditions was that the pro must be a single man. They had digs arranged for me above a local pub, but when they discovered I was not only married but also had a baby son, it all fell through. I recommended they sign my Petersham team-mate Ken Grieves, who fitted their requirements even though he had never bowled much. Ken was a young lad who had never strayed far from home and the prospect of crossing the oceans to seek his fame and fortune was slightly intimidating. But he went, married a Lancashire girl and to my knowledge did not even make a trip home for the best part of 35 years. Others were going by the boat-load. Cec Pepper, an exceptional player who played little or no first class cricket, Dooland, Jock Livingston and George Tribe all took up big offers to play in the leagues just as they emerged as real candidates for Test places.

I was in two minds. I was flattered by the interest being shown in me by people who had obviously never even seen my play, but while there was still a chance of playing for Australia I was reluctant to uproot my family and take such a huge step into the unknown.

A series of personal tragedies decided which way I was to turn, and when I say tragedies I cannot find any other way to describe what happened to me in the six most unhappy and traumatic months of my life. Even talking about it now stirs memories I would prefer to forget. My mother and my mother-in-law both died, and so too did my wife – in childbirth. In six short months I had lost everyone I had cared for; three of the people I had most loved and three of the people who had most loved me. I was a shattered and broken man. One such setback can hit any man hard. To have three – one after the other – is not the sort of thing you would wish on your worst enemy.

Now I'm a home-loving man and a family man and I need a home and family around me. To lose them all like that left me wondering what I had done to upset the Almighty. It was a series of experiences I hope I shall never live through again. The outcome was that I was alone in the world with a two year old son to support, a labouring job for my bread and butter and only the vague outside chance of a tour place to England. In the light of what I had been through it was very vague indeed. At nearly 30 years of age I had reached a turning point. What was I to do?

There did not seem much of a future for me in Australia. I pondered the Lancashire League offers from such strange-sounding places. They might just as well have been on another planet. Colne, a town divided by the Lancashire-Yorkshire border, came up with the best so far. They promised me a three year contract worth what was then a substantial amount of £500 a year with the added incentive that the hat would always be taken around among the crowd for a donation to the pro if he came up with the runs and the wickets expected of him. Some days this could amount to £40 or more. It was good money by any standards and so I sought advice. Bill O'Reilly, that marvellous servant of both New South Wales and Australia, had no doubts I should go. Stan McCabe, another great cricketer and an equally worldly-wise man, told me to stay. O'Reilly said with my talent I would go down well in the Lancashire leagues. He gave it to me straight: "Bill, even if you do get on the tour to England, you'll be lucky to get in the Test team. And when you return, what will there be here for you? You will be 30, with no special job and the memories of a string of personal tragedies to haunt you as you rebuild your life." Bill's advice rang true. He meant me well.

McCabe reckoned to wear the green baggy cap of Australia was worth any sacrifice. As an Australian, there could be no greater honour than to play for your country, and to throw away the chance when it was within your grasp, was little short of sacrilege. Once again, it was a viewpoint I had to consider.

For weeks I agonised over what to do. I realised that by going to England I was unlikely ever to be forgiven by the game's powers, especially in New South Wales, where they took a less tolerant attitude than other states like South Australia, where fortune-seekers like Dooland were forgiven and even played a few games on their return to the country. In short, though, I knew I was finished in Australia if I left its shores. On the other hand, there were better cricketers and bigger names in front of me in the queue for a Test place and my chances of forcing my way in were, realistically, slim. Had my personal circumstances been different I might have stayed, but events conspired against me, and with Colne more insistent than ever, I made a decision. I was on my way to England.

I suppose what made up my mind to leave Australia was the security of a three year contract. It was notoriously difficult to get a job in Australia that allowed you the time to develop as a cricketer. I remember what happened to Arthur Morris, an opening batsman fit to be ranked with best in any era. Morris was a civil servant and, after asking for five months off to go to England in 1948, he was asked to give an assurance he would be available for his work more often when he returned. When he told them he planned to carry on his cricket career, they promptly fired him. Finding a benevolent boss who gave you time off to pursue your sporting life was difficult, though some achieved it. But I never had any offer from home to stop me leaving for Colne.

I sometimes ponder what it must have been like to have played for my country. I have spent more of my life in England than I have in Australia, but I would have loved the opportunity of playing in a Test match, and the thought occurs to me more when I see some of the players lucky enough to have been selected over the years. Still, I stuck by my decision and I can honestly say, the missed Test cap aside, I have had absolutely no regrets about the move.

My main worry was my son, Ken. The poor little lad had just lost his mother and now he was about to lose me. Colne made it clear that the pro's job suited a single man and there was no way I could take Ken with me. My wife's sister and her husband solved the problem for me and I shall be grateful to them forever. They realised my dilemma and said, "Leave him with us". What a wonderful gesture, but it was with a heavy heart that I said goodbye to my boy and headed for England in the knowledge that it was likely to be three years – and possibly more – before I set eyes on him again. It is not an easy thing to do, turning your back on your own child, particularly so soon after his mother had died. In the event, even though I had a return boat ticket paid for by Colne Cricket Club in my pocket, it was indeed three years before I saw Ken again.

It was a crucial decision to leave all I knew and travel into the unknown. I had never left Australia, and the chances are I might never have done so if Irene had not died. In the event I am glad I did. It opened the door to 35 more years of the game I loved and a whole new way of life which I came to enjoy as much.

The cream of Australia's cricketing youth fled the shores at that time. Like me, they were lured to the leagues by big salaries and, like me, they were made to pay for it. I don't think we were ever forgiven by the Australian Board of Control. I can understand what it must have been like for those players who nailed their colours to Kerry Packer's mast. They were made to feel like lepers because they chose to make the best of their talent for the benefit of themselves and their families. I should imagine those West Indians who went to South Africa must have been subjected to the same sense of being rejected and scorned. I realise other factors were important in the case of the West Indies boys but the principle was the same. We were the first cricketing outcasts.

When I returned to the Sydney Cricket Ground in 1951-2 in my first visit home, I got a nasty shock. This was the ground, remember, which I had been proud to call my base for three seasons and on which I had twice scored a century in front of 30,000 crowds. But such was the sense of outrage still prevalent among the establishment that a gateman barred my entry. He told me in no uncertain terms that past services meant nothing. As far as he was concerned he had been told there was no way I was going to get in unless I produced a ticket. Can you imagine the humiliation? I had only been away three years but in their eyes I had ceased to exist. I stood at that gate wondering what the hell to do. My immediate reaction was to show my disgust by turning my back and walking away for ever. My pride was not going to let me pay – that was for sure. In the end I got a message taken to Keith Miller, who was playing in that match. Miller had to come down to the turnstile where I had been made to wait and give me a ticket to get in. Even then, my point proved, I nearly went home.

That incident just shows the bitterness and scars left by the exodus of talent to Lancashire and Yorkshire. It is not an incident I can readily forget; the pain will live with me to my dying day, and it is not – more than half a lifetime on – one I can easily forgive. Three or four of us, including Grieves and Pepper, made our homes in England, but the majority intended to return and did. But they had signed their own death warrants.

With so many players heading for England, it was little wonder that Australian domestic cricket began to decline after the high point of Bradman's 1948 tour party. Grade matches were played at near-deserted grounds and it was some time before a new batch of young talent emerged. As a man labelled a "traitor" it gave me no great satisfaction to learn of the falling standards.

One of my last acts in grade cricket in Sydney was to end the distinguished career of Stan McCabe, whose advice I had chosen to ignore – though not because I did not trust him. Stan was playing for Mosman against Petersham and it was fair to say he was on the verge of retirement anyway. He had just returned from injury and was still feeling his way back to form. With the first ball of the match he pushed forward at me and I bowled him through the gate. The ignominy of being knocked over by me was too much for the old chap. "That's it," he said as he came off. "If Bill Alley can bowl me then it's time to go". With that, he took off his pads and to my knowledge never played a competitive game of cricket again.

It is curious how time changes your priorities. For many years as a young cricketer in Sydney and in Brooklyn, short of actually playing for your country, the best most of us could aspire to was wearing the light blue and white jumpers of New South Wales and, of course, the light blue cap. It was a symbol of achievement and I wore mine proudly. Yet in the early 1980's I was standing as an umpire in a festival match at Hastings. Allan Border was playing in the match but I didn't know him from Adam. When he came on to bowl he handed me this jumper of his and I knew I had seen something similar before. Allan was playing for New South Wales in those days and it was their jumper he gave me to look after while he bowled. Out of context, I didn't recognise it. I said to him, "Which team is this?" He looked at me in astonishment. "You ought to know", he told me, "You bloody played for them". He was right. I should have known. But it had been many years since my battles for and against the New South Wales Cricket Association and a lot of water had passed under the bridge.

3
Into Exile

AS WHAT IS PROBABLY the greatest team ever to leave the shores of Australia was being assembled in 1948 for the triumphant tour of England, I was packing my own bags for the lonely trip into exile at Colne. Even the simple task of getting my belongings from Australia went hopelessly wrong. Anyone who has ever travelled on a boat from Australia to England will know it is a long, boring trip and a sharp contrast to the 24-hour jets of today. I tried to keep myself fit on board as the ship made its slow progress away from all I had known.

When I got to Tilbury Docks on a cold Spring day there was more than just the weather to send a chill down my spine. All my trunks into which I had placed everything I owned in life had been smashed open. All that was left of treasured belongings were a dressing gown, a pair of thick pyjamas and two cricket bats. The "wharfies" at Sydney harbour had helped themselves to the rest. The newspapers were full of stories about players like me deserting and I can only think that they were as good as a tip-off. With my name and destination plastered all over the trunks, these guys obviously thought they would have a look at what I was taking with me. Maybe it was a curious act of compassion which forced them to spare my dressing gown and pyjamas for the colder climes of England. I rather think they came to the conclusion that neither garment was of any use to them. As for the bats, I will never know why they were left untouched. In a strange sort of way it was Australia's final act of revenge on me. No matter, the deed had been done and it was one of the grimmest experiences of my life, standing on the dock of a strange country having discovered virtually all my possessions had gone for ever.

It gives me some satisfaction to realise now that I would not have got into that all-conquering team of Bradman's in 1948. To have forced my way into the 17-strong touring party would have been remarkable in itself, yet outstanding players like Colin McCool and Doug Ring went to England and hardly got a look-in. It galled me a bit to think that first summer in Lancashire that, elsewhere in England, Ernie Toshack was wearing my shirts in the name of Australia – but it gives me a chuckle when I recall it now. Toshack was a magnet for the girls with his 6 ft 2 inch frame and his dark good looks and he acquired a bit of a reputation as a womaniser. Those of us who knew him were reduced to tears of laughter when the official tour brochure described him as an office worker "with fifteen women under him". He claimed, of course, it was no exaggeration!

It was a strange experience swapping the warmth and open spaces of Australia for the industrial landscape of northern England, with its chimney pots and drab little houses. I could not understand how people could live in such cramped conditions, but I soon came to love the warm, open-hearted attitude of Colne's inhabitants. My first game in the Lancashire League was played in a snow storm and the coldness of the first few days made me grateful to those Sydney wharfies for allowing me to keep my warm pyjamas.

I flung myself into this weird form of cricket with all these big name professionals from Australia, India and the West Indies leading packs of Saturday afternoon cricketers, among whom the standard varied considerably. I also flung myself into a social whirl in a bid to fill the large gap left in my life by Irene's death. I had intended to bring a girl with me from Australia but her mother disapproved of me. By her reckoning I may have been a widower but I was also a married man, and she did all she could to end our relationship. In the end she succeeded. Alone in a foreign country I wrote to this girl regularly and fully expected her to follow me to England eventually. But unknown to me her mother was laying her hands on my letters first and then disposing of them before my girlfriend could ever set eyes on them. I could never understand why she

23

didn't write back. She, in turn, thought I had met someone else and the relationship quietly died.

Luckily, I soon had a massive stroke of good fortune. I met Betty, the woman who was to become my second wife and who has been the inspiration of my life ever since. Betty was a telephonist in her home town of Rawtenstall, not far from Colne, and we were first introduced at a dance. I had only been in the country for two weeks but I knew straight away that she was the girl for me. I am ashamed to admit it was three months before I plucked up the courage to ask her out. She got a tremendous shock when I rang the exchange and, instead of asking for a number, invited her out instead. Even then she didn't agree to my request immediately. She was sure I was married because there was a rumour to that effect circulating the town. She even sought advice from a friend before confronting me with the question: "Are you married?". I told her I had been but my first wife had died. It was only then she agreed to start a relationship which is as strong today as it was 12 months later when we married.

When I first came to Colne I was placed in digs with a rather large woman by the name of Miss Lord. When I say large I mean it. She must have been 20 stone and she saw it as her job not only to feed me, but also to look after my moral welfare. The overseas professional, I soon discovered, had a prestigious position within the community. This was in the days before mass immigration of Indians, Pakistanis and other cultures to the industrial cities of northern England and a foreign accent was something of an oddity and an object of curiosity. I have to admit I had a job understanding their Lancashire accents and it was all like a foreign language. Somehow I got by and before long fan letters from young ladies started to fall on the mat of my digs. I was flattered to say the least. Miss Lord was far from amused and made her disapproval known to me, not that it was my fault. When I started courting Betty, Miss Lord hardly spoke to me for weeks. I am convinced she thought I was still married and was taking advantage of Betty, but I don't suppose I shall ever discover the truth.

My involvement with Betty Cortman prevented me from using my return ticket to Australia that winter. Instead I stayed on to work on Colne's sloping Horsfield ground as its groundsman, one of only three winters in the next 36 in which I have been forced to find employment out of simple economic necessity. For the rest of my cricket career I have been lucky enough to have the privilege of loafing around at home in a sort of hibernation, and it is when I consider that fact I come to realise how fortunate I have been.

The following year, 1949, I married Betty at St. Paul's Church, Constable Lee, where an old cricketing friend from Australia, Jack Pettiford, was best man and I can honestly say it was one of the best moves of my life. We had a honeymoon in Scarborough and in a matter of days I was off to India, Pakistan and Ceylon with a Commonwealth touring party made up of professionals from all over the world. It was hardly the ideal way to start married life but Betty forgave me and now I shudder to think what I would do without her. She means so much to me. For the last 50 years she has never stood in my way as cricket took priority and she has been obliged to stay at home bringing up our family, hardly seeing me for months on end. I must have been on ten or eleven overseas tours in the English winters and then came all those long summers when I was away with Somerset or umpiring. She has never complained and for that I am eternally grateful.

I might appear to be the archetypal Australian to some people; big, bluff, straight-talking. I will admit now to being more sensitive than I might sometimes seem. It is a statement of fact when I tell you I have twice seriously considered taking my own life. I am not seeking sympathy, nor am I ashamed to admit it. When my first wife died the thought often occurred to me that it would be simpler to end it all by jumping in front of a train – or something, I'm not sure what. I reasoned I had nothing to live for; everything I had ever loved had been snatched away from me. The night-time was the worst. The long hours of darkness when all fears seemed exaggerated and my misery was at its most intense. I could not see much point in going on because my world had collapsed around

25

me. Luckily I snapped out of this dreadful depression and got over it, probably when I realised I had a young son to look after.

I am an emotional man. I cry easily if I see something on television which moves me. The sad decline of Muhammad Ali, for instance, can bring the tears welling up. I looked at the way people I had known so well in my lifetime had declined, like Bill Voce, the former Nottinghamshire and England bowler, and the Lord's groundsman Jim Fairbrother, who died so soon after retirement, and I wondered what would happen to me. Before my last season as an umpire I wondered if I would even get through that season. Over the years both my kneecaps have been taken off; the wear and tear of a sportsman's life had taken their toll and it was while I was waiting to enter hospital to have 360 pounds worth of steel put into one of my knees that I endured the most terrible pain. Artificial joints now operate instead of my knee caps and arthritis has set in. As I rested at my home on the outskirts of Taunton for the hospital to call me in, I came close once more to the dark thoughts of suicide. I kept a gun to shoot rabbits which strayed on to my two-acre smallholding. I was in agony and Betty knew it. She sensed my moods were getting blacker and she hid the gun from me. It was a wise precaution and shows how much I have come to depend on her over the years. It only takes a bit of courage to pull that trigger, and I often contemplated it as the pain grew more intense and I grew more desperate to be rid of it. Even now, if anything happened to Betty I wonder what I would do.

I am sorry to have sounded so melancholy but this was how I felt and it is only right that I use this opportunity to tell the truth.

Betty and I soon had two young children of our own. Douglas and Timothy were both born in Lancashire and now live near us in Somerset. Both have had the good sense to avoid a career in professional cricket but, as befitting the sons of Bill Alley, retain an interest in the game. Our family was completed when in 1951-2 I went home to Sydney to collect Ken from my former sister-in-law. I cannot remember ever being as nervous as when Betty and I called round to see him. After all, I had left him when he was little more than a baby, and there was no way of telling how he would react to meeting me after all this time. There was a little, worrying pause; then he leapt into my arms. We were reunited and there was no happier man in Sydney as I put behind me the dreadful sequence of disasters which haunted my final years in Australia. My sister-in-law had always told Ken I would return to pick him up one day and he came gladly when I went back to Colne. He had a rough time when he started to adjust to life in Lancashire. At school his classmates used to tease him about his Aussie accent and he got himself into an endless succession of scrapes. Suddenly he lost his Australian "language" and began to speak with as broad a Lancastrian accent as you could find and he was accepted by his mates as one of them at last.

Ken was a useful cricketer, and after trials with Somerset I had high hopes he might make a living out of the game and to share the tremendous experiences I had gathered from my many years in cricket. But it was not to be. He joined the Army instead and soon came to enjoy life in the services. He was 25, engaged to be married and with a full and happy life to look forward to when tragedy struck once more. It was 1970 and a tank in which he was travelling in West Germany overturned in a freak accident. Ken was one of two soldiers on board incinerated in the fire which broke out when the tank went over. I came home late that night from the ground at Taunton to find a telegram and a sobbing family waiting for me. "I regret to inform you, your son has been killed", it said in words to that effect. Apparently the tank had struck a stationary car. Not for the first time in my life, I was thunder-struck with grief and sorrow. I sometimes wonder if my first marriage was fated in some bizarre way. Whatever, Betty, who had brought up Ken as if he was her own son, helped me pick myself up and life somehow got back to normal. In the gloom of the funeral, and the tears of his bereaved fiancée, I wondered what the hell was going to happen next.

All that was in the future, but back in the early days I could not get used to Colne's little ground in the first few weeks after I arrived from Australia. Nor could I get over the strange wickets with the ball moving all over the place. I will admit to having some lingering hopes that Bradman's tourists would be struck down with an injury or two and a call would be made summoning me as a replacement, but it never came, and it was made clear subsequently that none of the defectors would have been forgiven and brought in from the cold of league cricket. My chance had gone and I knew it and I resolved to make the best of my new and strange environment. League cricket took some understanding. I was accustomed to going miles without seeing another soul in some parts of Australia. In Lancashire there were all these little communities packed into a small area and yet never mingling. I soon discovered it was important for the professional to be successful. The whole town depended on him.

When I arrived at Colne the club chairman, Frank Wilson, made it absolutely clear what was expected of me. I was to score 80 or 90 runs at least every time I went out to bat and five wickets every time I bowled. The hat was taken around for the pro once he reached his fifty and again if he took six wickets or more. It was a tall order, but the crowds, which were often between 3,000 and 4,000, soon came to love my style of batting. I don't think I let them down very often, but the people of Colne had their ways of letting me know if they thought I had failed them. If I had done well the previous Saturday I only had to enter a pub and there was a rush to buy me a drink. Others would shake my hand in the street and car horns would sound as I walked in happy recognition of my weekend achievements. But fail them, boy, and you were in trouble! If the unthinkable happened and I was out cheaply and Colne lost, I was in the proverbial dog-house for seven days until I could redeem myself. They took defeat badly and I was the scapegoat. I bought my own drinks and turned up my coat collar.

I like to think I came to terms with the requirements quickly, but some other big names imported from abroad struggled to match the new demands on their talents. Frank Worrell, Clyde Walcott and Everton Weekes all made a living from the leagues in those days, and they were the men I always had to get out – and was expected to get out. They had no problems living up to their star billing, but even spin bowlers were expected to open their team's innings and to get runs, no matter if they were genuine tail-enders in first class cricket. Some teams had outstanding amateur players but it was usually a question of which of the two opposing professionals was most successful on the day.

The main object of league matches was to keep the professional away from the amateur bowlers. They would be offered singles to keep them out of the firing line, but a seasoned professional knew when to refuse them. It was a tremendous weekly battle of wits between players of international standing and the outcome of the match usually depended on which of them won their personal battle. Every precaution was taken to make sure a visiting professional did not perform on a wicket suitable to his talents. If a top-class seamer was due at Horsfield, we spent the previous seven days cutting every blade of grass the moment it poked its head above ground. If a spinner was our next major opponent, we let it all grow so that it was hard to tell the wicket from the rest of the playing area.

I was told when I first arrived by a schoolteacher that they "diddle you out", and I knew what he meant when in my first match I was bowled leg stump by a ball which must have spun back 18 inches. If I needed a lesson in the way the ball moved in English conditions, then that was it. I resolved to tighten my defence, and the first thing I did from then on was to make sure my leg stump was well covered by my pad. Most cricketers brought up on hard and fast wickets will acknowledge, as I did, how playing in the leagues improved their defensive technique. I like to think I became a much better player for my eight years in Lancashire by adding to my natural aggression a mean streak. It was a question of necessity. I realised from the start that the team – and the town – depended on me to win them matches and that meant compiling big scores. There was no use lifting my head and clouting half a dozen sixes in a fast and furious fifty if the opposition's professional was taking his time over a match-winning century. My living relied on my ability to score as many runs as possible, and I became a far more reliable player as a result.

I spent five happy years at Colne, during which we had our measure of success in league and cup matches, and I broke all records once I had adjusted to the demands of the type of cricket. With collections I must have been making more than £1,000 a season, which was better money than many county players could expect, and I was free in the winter to do as I pleased. What is more, on Sundays during the cricket season when I was not on duty for Colne, the vast number of Australians formed themselves into a sort of touring troupe and big crowds came to watch us all around the north. It was enjoyable and lucrative, but Colne's "never on a Sunday" ruling began to irritate me and was the signal for the beginning of the end to a marvellous relationship.

My irritation about not being allowed to play on Sundays as frequently as I would have liked, and one or two minor grouses, led to me expressing my dissatisfaction in no uncertain terms. The word got round Colne that Bill Alley was ready to pack his bags and a public meeting was called. The Town Hall was filled and my future was hotly debated. But it was too late. I had made up my mind to join Blackpool in the Northern League and I was on my way again.

Just before I left Colne, Somerset made me an offer but I rejected it quickly, much as I had done other county overtures. At the time I was under contract to Colne, happily settled in Lancashire with a locally born wife and two young children, and in my mid-30s I was reluctant to take a chance in county cricket. It was not that I doubted my ability, but the thought of playing cricket six days a week put me off.

The nearest I came to taking up one of those offers was when Lancashire summoned me to Old Trafford after I had been at Colne for three years. Old Trafford is one of England's biggest grounds and the thought of playing for Lancashire was a tempting one. But it all turned sour when I was confronted by the Lancashire coach, Harry Makepeace. The offer was a good one and I was convinced I would sign. Then Harry suggested I was too aggressive for county cricket. He told me I would need to change my style and learn to play off the back foot more. I was staggered by his attitude, grabbed the contract from his hands, and in a great show of disdain, tore it into four pieces and flushed it down the nearest lavatory. Harry and the Lancashire committee were stunned into silence and I promptly left the ground without another word being said.

Gloucestershire also made me an offer which included £5 from a weekly newspaper column, but I was so well paid by Colne that I never took it seriously. Warwickshire, Northamptonshire, Nottinghamshire and Kent all made it clear that age may be against me as a long-term prospect but I could still do a useful job for them. Kent and Nottinghamshire both set up highly interesting deals after I had moved to Blackpool, but each time I pulled out at the last minute. Neither club had told me what I wanted to hear.

Nottinghamshire were willing to give me £750 a season, a house and a winter job. For the first time I could see no real reason why I should not step up to county cricket. Once more I was on the verge of saying "yes" when they told me I would probably be batting at six or seven. This hurt my pride and I backed out of negotiations as Kent made a counter-offer. They promised me I would be opening the innings with Arthur Fagg and this seemed a much better proposition. I think I had made up my mind that if I was to leave the security of league cricket, where I was not only highly successful but also extremely well paid, then it would be to go to Kent. One evening I received a call from a former Kent committee man who made it clear I would not go down well in such a "patrician" county as Kent. As an outsider, I would not be easily accepted, he told me. This caller refused to give his name but his words were enough to sow the seeds of doubt in my mind and, yet again, I brought an end to any speculation that I was leaving Blackpool.

Blackpool were the strongest team in a weak league and in the four years I played for them I ended up with an average of more than 100. It was a comfortable way to make a good living and, despite the flow of county offers, I was not prepared to swap this for the insecurity of full-time professional cricket. I was as much a celebrity in Blackpool as soccer players like Stanley Matthews and Ernie Taylor. I bought a smart house near the sea and was fairly certain I would end my playing career in a place I had grown to like and where I was readily appreciated. Matthews and I became firm friends and we even trained together.

He was a dedicated sportsman, always doing more work than the other players and setting himself a high standard of fitness. I remember there was a benefit match for me one summer at Blackpool's Stanley Park and some of the footballers turned out on my behalf. But Matthews refused to be involved. He told me he would have no part of a game in which he would be seen to be less than excellent. He, too, had his pride. I suggested he might be kind enough to take a collection box around the ground for me. The mere mention of it turned him pale. He was far too shy to go among the crowd. The thought genuinely scared him. From anyone else I would have looked upon his attitude as a badly disguised way of opting out, but Stan was like that. He was a timid man and a great footballer, but he wanted nothing to do with anything which would expose him to the public glare.

To their credit, Somerset never gave up the chase. Harold Stephenson, their wicketkeeper, had been following my progress for years and, even though I was now approaching the veteran stage, he managed to persuade his cricket committee to make me an offer. It was not as good as the one Nottinghamshire had made me earlier. Somerset were not one of the richer counties, but it was good enough to get me thinking. From what I can recall, Somerset told me I could have £800 a year, a club house and a testimonial at the end of my three year contract. I was very tempted. Blackpool, like most league clubs, had a policy of taking on their professionals one season at a time. I had been there four years but there was no question of a long-term contract. I put it to Tom Bradley, the Blackpool chairman, that if they could match Somerset's terms I would stay. The Blackpool committee called my bluff. They stuck to their policy. At the age of 38, at a time when other players were thinking of hanging up their boots, I got into my car and made the long journey to the West Country and signed the papers which opened the door to yet anther whole new way of life. It was the start of my third career in cricket.

Had Blackpool even come close to equalling Somerset's bid then I am sure I would have taken the easy way out and stayed at Stanley Park. There was no need for me to go, but Somerset represented some form of security when they offered me a long-term contract. I was not desperate to leave Blackpool, but with three young children to support I was convinced I had made the right decision. Even so, on the drive home I could not help wondering what I had let myself in for. It was all very well to be averaging over 100 in club cricket, but that was achieved among amateurs intent upon enjoying themselves in the fresh air. Now I had committed myself to taking on international class cricketers every day of the week, and to a punishing schedule of travelling the length and breadth of England in the days before motorways were any more than a planner's dream. I had agreed to become a professional among professionals, all with a living to make, and, as a foreigner with little first-class experience behind me, it was a daunting prospect stepping up at a time when I was no longer in the first flush of youth.

Somerset was a long way from anything I had previously known, even in England. In the nine years since I had arrived from Australia, Lancashire's homely little towns were all I had been familiar with. The rolling green fields of Somerset seemed strange to me. It was a bit like emigrating all over again, especially as they appeared to speak in a totally foreign tongue. I am pleased to say it is a move I have never regretted. On the contrary, it was the best I ever made.

Financial aspects aside, one of the reasons I joined Somerset was because I simply liked the name. It had a nice ring about it; I don't know why. Unlike people brought up in England, I had no concept of the place before I moved there. I did not know about the cider or the beautiful countryside. Nor had I come across the magnificent accent of its inhabitants. No, I can honestly say that a major contributing cause to my uprooting my family was the sheer magic of the name, Somerset. For the same reason, I could not have signed for Hampshire. I didn't like the sound of the county, though I knew nothing of them as a club whatsoever. I am glad also I did not agree to move to either Warwickshire or Sussex. I could not have played for either with their ridiculous badges plastered over their jumpers. Those birds – Martlets, I think they are called – which represent the Sussex motif, have always struck me as strange, to say the least. When I was an umpire and Sussex players handed me their jumpers I used to say "How can you wear this?". As for Warwickshire, their badge has a bear on it holding on to what looks like a tree. Need I say more?

4
My Indian Summer

I HAD THREE YEARS to prove myself when I joined Somerset in 1957, at the advanced age of 38, and I could hardly have made a worse start. We were playing old rivals Gloucestershire soon after my debut and I had scored only eight when I hoisted a leg side delivery straight down Martin Young's throat at fine leg. The rivalry between the two counties has always been intense, more so then than now. I can tell you it was a long walk back to the crowded and silent pavilion. The Somerset supporters must have wondered what they had let themselves in for. Here was this trumped-up Aussie with thousands of runs under his belt, scored against amateurs, hailed as a saviour by the county committee, and now out in the most amateurish manner. I had just reached the pavilion when I heard someone shout, "Send him back on the next boat. He'll be no good for Somerset". Others were doubtless sharing his view as I made my lonely way up to the dressing-room. But I resolved there and then to prove them wrong. I had staked my reputation and the welfare of my family on this belated break into first-class cricket and I had no intention of failing. I was determined to play my game, and if that meant being caught on the boundary going for a big hit, then so be it. I had been given three years by Somerset and if it took me the entire length of my contract, I was determined to succeed eventually.

Somerset were a strange outfit in those days. We were a happy and largely ineffective contrast to counties like Kent, Lancashire, Yorkshire and the all-conquering Surrey. They played to win because it was expected of them; we also played to win, but we hardly ever did, so we contented ourselves with enjoying the game as much as possible. Any fears I might have had about being accepted quickly evaporated. I had every right to feel self-conscious about my age

35

and about my lack of real experience of first-class cricket. I had made the big choice to uproot my family to a different part of the country and I was worried as to how it would all work out. It is easy enough to move when you are single and young, as I had been when I left Australia, but it was another matter making a decision when the lives of the people who mattered most to me were also being affected.

Our team was an odd mixture of other counties' rejects and itinerant overseas players. Colin McCool and John McMahon were other Australians who had been lured to English cricket's western outpost, and it was no surprise that we became known as a "League of Nations" team. Curiously enough for such an unusual concoction, we had a team spirit second to none. While other teams fretted away worrying about the destination of championships, we were content to earn a reputation as the best social team in the country. My word, how we enjoyed ourselves! Long after our opponents had sloped off to their hotels or home, we were drinking seriously, often into the small hours.

I thought nothing of knocking back six or seven pints of black and tan, a tasty little habit I had acquired in the north, and then getting stuck into the gin and tonics. I found it no problem to wash down the black and tans (which, for those of you who do not know, is brown and mild bitter beer mixed) with another half dozen gin and tonics, and there was never even the suggestion of a hangover the next day when battle was resumed on the field of play in earnest. If my game had in any way been affected I would have given it all up there and then, but, on the contrary, if anything it was improved for my nightly intake of alcohol. Some nights I used to cut out the beer altogether. Then I limited myself to 15 or 20 gin and tonics and the company of many good mates in the Somerset team. I can promise you this is no exaggeration. We all did it and no one was the worse for wear the next day. I drank for the friendship of my new teammates and in the winter hardly drank at all, except at functions. This does not imply that we took our jobs lightly. We realised we were fortunate to be making a living out of something we enjoyed doing and we always knew when to stop – and that, very often, was at about midnight.

My worries subsided when Somerset affirmed their faith in me by awarding me my county cap after ten innings and 365 runs. It was a particularly pleasing moment because a cap is a symbol of recognition and it is not usually given lightly. From that moment I began to relax and enjoy life in rural Somerset and, I am pleased to say, am still doing so today. The Somerset people are as easy-going as I was led to believe and, when I first started playing for the county way back in 1957, so too were the players. I realised I had made the right decision and I went flat out to get the best of what I thought was the Indian summer of my career. Time alone showed it was really only the start.

I was no longer, and I doubt whether I had been, the swiftest thing on two legs in the field, but I had always possessed a good pair of hands and I adapted myself into a gully fieldsman. I like to think there were few specialist gullies to compare with me while I was playing for Somerset, and my high tally of catches – nearly 300 in my career – would tend to support my boast. My catching was a further string to my bow, but I also had my batting and my medium-paced bowling to help keep me involved every minute of a three-day county match.

As I have said, I was a negative sort of bowler because I did not have the genuine pace to blast anyone out, least of all top county cricketers, many of whom would be Test players. I was the sort of bowler who wouldn't give his grandmother a full toss on her birthday, and it gave me as much pleasure to bowl a maiden to class batsmen like Tom Graveney and Colin Cowdrey than to actually take the wicket of a lesser batsman. I regarded it as a moral victory to stop great players from scoring and with the use of length and line, honed by nine years in the Lancashire leagues, I played on tiny weaknesses in the armoury of the outstanding and I worked away until I won. Even so, my bowling resources and skills were tested rather more than I had anticipated and I earned my money with plenty of work. This was because Somerset never had a bowler so fast that the opposition were worried. There were plenty like me who could turn our arms over at medium pace or slightly above, but no one to scare the pants off the other counties. We had no one to take wickets by speed alone and, for that reason, we came to be regarded as easy pickings for the stronger clubs, some of whom, like Surrey in the days of Laker, Lock and Peter May, were as good as Test teams.

Yorkshire, too, with Fred Trueman in his prime, were another team to be feared and I'm afraid to say it was just a question of how long we could last against them. In my first season it was not uncommon for us to be turned over in two days, or at best two and a half, but we never lost our sense of fun and I like to think we enjoyed our game rather more than our conquerors, particularly, as I recall, Surrey. One of the good things about our inability to bowl out the better sides twice was that this usually meant we always had two knocks of our own. This may help to account for my 1540 runs in my debut season. No matter, we became accustomed to long periods of defence, since it was the only way we could be sure of avoiding defeat, and in my early days this was always Somerset's priority. Anything else was very much a bonus until 1958 when we finished third.

Some times we took our social activity too far. We were playing Glamorgan in Cardiff and the woman hotelier had long taken a fancy to Brian Lobb, one of the Somerset players. Unfortunately for her, Brian did not reciprocate her affections. On the contrary, I think it fair to say he positively loathed the thought of her and his embarrassment was plain to see every time we set up camp at the hotel. One day he came up with a ruse to end her starry-eyed interest in him once and for all. He went out and bought three herrings and, carefully cutting them up, draped pieces over light bulbs. Of course, every time the lights were turned on the herrings began to cook and before long the hotel reeked of the most awful odour from top to bottom. It was long after we had departed that the poor woman found out the cause, and I wonder how many customers she must have lost in the meantime! Brian was well pleased with his work and I'm pretty certain she never saw him in quite the same way again.

Most of our other pranks were far less hazardous and we all revelled in the homely, easy atmosphere which was more akin to a club side than a professional county. Betty met the other wives three times a week for coffee at a restaurant named "Maynard's" in Taunton and benefit matches, which were then played on Sundays, were family affairs with the children coming along to join in the fun. In the winter we played mixed skittles with other team members and their wives and, in general, it was a good and happy club of which to be part. In those days the club owned a dozen or more houses and when we first moved down from Lancashire we lived in one of them. The players used to meet in the Crown and Sceptre in Taunton every night of the week when we were not playing and our social life always seemed to involve other Somerset cricketers.

Looking back now I realise how much this was all planned by our skipper, Maurice Tremlett. Maurice died prematurely in 1984, but, having studied all the great captains from Bradman down to Brearley and watched them from close quarters, I reckon Maurice was the best of the lot. He knew our limitations better than anyone and, acknowledging a big gap in talent between ourselves and some of the other counties, resolved to build a team spirit second to none. And in my estimation he succeeded.

If Maurice had been blessed with some outstanding, match-winning bowlers then I am sure he would have had the recognition he deserved. Instead, I imagine he will only truly be remembered within the boundaries of Somerset, and even then his achievements swamped by what Richards, Botham and Co have managed since. Maurice did not have those sort of resources at his disposal and it was a miracle when in 1958 he led his happy band of jokers to third place in the county championship, the highest position they had ever reached. Maurice earned himself three caps for England as an all-rounder but, for no reason that we could ever discover, suddenly lost the ability to bowl. From what I can make out it was some sort of psychological block. In the nets he could be a devastating bowler, but he fell to pieces when he was obliged to pitch a decent length and line on the field of play. To the end he could never explain what had happened or where he had gone wrong, but it did not stop him developing a shrewd approach to captaincy, which was designed to get the best out of an ageing bunch of mercenaries.

We became intensely loyal to Maurice and he never abused our faith in him. In 1958 we shrugged aside our label as a sociable crowd of second-raters and the bigger counties, brimming with big names, were forced to treat us with a respect they had not always shown when I first came down two years before. I am convinced that if we had been able to field a Joel Garner or a Malcolm Marshall we would have won the championship. We were never in a position to rip out the opposition and Maurice could only force a result by astute declarations, sometimes twice in a match. In 1958 we had a batting line up to match the best in England, but the bowling was built around the likes of me, wheeling away for 58 wickets at just over 23 runs each. How we longed for a man of sheer pace to go through the opposition – and how well we did to get so far without one. Maurice had an amazing capacity to time his declarations to perfection, and what victories we achieved that summer were the result of his ability to set a target which teased the opposition into reckless sacrifice, or by other captains under-estimating our batting strength. I am pleased to say I played my part with 1318 runs at 23.53 and I only wish our combined efforts had produced greater reward, for the sake of Maurice Tremlett.

I was loving every minute of life in Somerset and there was nothing I enjoyed more than personal duels with the top players of the day. At Yeovil in 1960, on a wicket where it was almost impossible to score a run, I bowled 15.3 successive maidens at Trevor Bailey as Essex clung on desperately for a draw. The ball was lifting viciously off a length but Trevor got his head down, as only he could, and defied us in one of the gutsiest performances I ever came across. The Somerset record for successive maidens was 16, but I had no idea I was even close to it as I tried everything I knew to dig him out. Then in the 16th over he was dropped close to the wicket by Roy Virgin and I think, for the first time, he became a little rattled. Next ball he lobbed me in a rather panicky fashion into the outfield and scampered two rather fortunate runs. But credit to him, Trevor recovered his poise, went back into his shell, and we had to be content with a draw when a win looked certain. I'm told he batted two hours ten minutes for 14 not out.

Tom Graveney was another man with whom I had some fascinating battles. I had not realised how much Gloucestershire players were disliked by Somerset supporters, and in Tom they had a batsman with whom they had every reason to fear. Many a time he dispatched what I thought were excellent deliveries with effortless ease to the boundary. The Somerset president wanted him out of the way so much he offered a bonus of £2 to the bowler who got him out. I never needed much incentive to try my hardest against Tom, although the extra two quid made his wicket all the more precious. Anyway, I studied Tom and came to the conclusion he sometimes played too early at a slower delivery and, if you were lucky, he might spoon a catch to mid-on or mid-off. I was talking over my theory to my teammates before Tom was due to go out to bat. His brother Ken, still a prominent name in Gloucestershire ranks, must have overheard me, but by then Tom was at the crease. Sure enough, Tom lifted a gentle catch to mid-on off my slower delivery before he had got into his stride. As we came off at the end of the session, Ken ran down the steps to greet me. And he wasn't smiling when he wagged his finger at me and said "You old fox!" I laughed. I was just about to become two pounds richer. It has to be said, though, that this was a rare success against a player I came to rate highly.

Tremlett moved on and we never repeated our success of 1958. In 1960 I failed by a couple of hundred runs to hit a thousand, but I am pleased to report that 1960 and 1965 were the only years I did not chalk up four figures in a season. I suppose there must have been one or two people in Somerset and beyond who must have been thinking age had caught up with me at last, that at 41 I was over the hill. How wrong they were. The next season, 1961, was the most successful of my career, and it all coincided with the testimonial I had been promised as part of the deal which brought me down from Blackpool.

Many cricketers struggle during their benefit or testimonial years because of the sheer weight of organising events and then attending them. In my case it was the opposite. Everything seemed to click into place, and at the end of it I had 3,019 runs and 62 wickets against my name - plus another 29 catches, most of them in my favourite gully position. During my golden season I scored two centuries against Richie Benaud's visiting Australians and was five runs short of scoring a third.

In all I scored eleven centuries and ten fifties and ended up with an average of 56.96. Remember, I was now 42 and by most standards supposed to be heading for my cricketing dotage, but I had never felt fitter in my life and was determined to make up for lost time. It was not as though I felt I had anything to prove, either to myself or those who might have thought I had reached the end of the line. I believe the previous three or four years had hardened me to the needs of county cricket, to the long days in the field and to the wearisome travelling. At 42 I was in my prime and I have never enjoyed myself more.

I am proud to say I was the last player in English cricket to score more than 3,000 runs in a season and now that the number of fixtures has been cut back to accommodate the limited overs competitions, it will need a run machine to beat my record. Not only was I successful on the field, but my testimonial provided a great boost to my finances and I picked up a cheque for more than £2,000, which was a lot of money in those days, and which was enough to enable me to buy my bungalow at Adsborough near Taunton with its two acres for my sheep and chickens. The public of Somerset had come to like me and my style of play and they gave willingly from their pockets. For that I shall always be grateful.

Before the start of the 1961 season a doctor asked to see me. I thought at the time he wanted to examine me to disprove my claim that I was only 42. Instead he said: "Bill, I want you to become a guinea-pig.". I wondered what on earth he was talking about. Before I could decline and retreat to the bar, he made me an offer. He said: "I want you to take three of these pills every day during the summer". I asked him what was in them and what they were supposed to do to me. He would not tell me. "Don't worry," he assured me, "They will help your game and at the end of the summer I will reveal what they are made of." For some reason, I agreed to his suggestion and with that he melted into the background. For all I knew they might have been some home-made cure for gout. But he had insisted they would improve my performance and I went along with it. Apparently these pills were not on the market but he wanted to see if they worked.

Looking back on it, I should have pressed him into telling me what they were supposed to do to me apart from improve my performance. He could have been wanting to turn me into a junkie, but just to go along with his ruse I dutifully dipped my hand into the jar and took three each day of the season. My teammates thought it was some kind of youth preservative I was tipping down my throat, but eleven centuries and 3,000 runs later it was me who was having the last laugh. The funny thing is, I can honestly say I have never felt fitter or stronger in my life than I did that year and I am left to conclude it was all down to a doctor's prescription. That and the black and tans! If I had been in my right mind I would have given them up but the pills seemed to bring me luck and success and, as much as anything, they became a sort of superstition. They didn't seem to give me wondrous powers but I was reluctant to consign them to the dustbin in case my game fell apart. I was "hooked" on a jar of tablets and I didn't dare tell anyone outside the club.

Anyway, at the end of the season this doctor, who was a well-known Somerset member and still practices near Bristol, came forward. "What was in them, Doc?" I asked. "I'd like to tell you but I can't", he replied. I was hardly in a position to get angry after the greatest five months of my career, but I pleaded with him to tell me. He nodded his head. "It was an experiment, Bill, and you were the guinea-pig, as I had asked you to be. Perhaps one day I will put you out of your misery". To this day I have never known what was in those tablets. Was it a psychological ploy? Or did they really contain something which lifted my powers beyond the normal? Whatever, the record books say Bill Alley had his best summer and they don't say anything about a jar of tablets.

The tablets aside, 1961 was a season when everything went right. I set a new county record and in ten extraordinary days in the middle of June scored 523 runs for only once out with three centuries. I could do no wrong. I suppose most players have little spells when they see the ball like the proverbial football and when they feel nothing, short of a bomb, can blast them out of the batting crease. Surrey might not have been the power they had been in the 1950s but they were still a strong side and could never be taken lightly. Even so, I scored 183 not out and 134 not out against them at Taunton to become the first Somerset player to notch up a pair of not out centuries in the same match, and followed that with an unbeaten 150 against them at the Oval. I ended with an aggregate of 476 from our two meetings with Surrey and they never got me out. Just to rub their noses in it, I grabbed eight for 65 the next year against them, which was to be my best ever return in first-class cricket.

Surrey were not the only county to run into Bill Alley at his best. Against Warwickshire at Nuneaton I hit six sixes and 31 fours in an unbeaten 221 – and I still finished on the losing side!

Ken Palmer, another Somerset player who went on to become a Test umpire, helped me create a new county record for the sixth wicket when we put on 265 in less than four hours against Northamptonshire at Northampton. Yet another Somerset record tumbled when I scored my eighth century of the season, against Essex at Weston, beating that jointly held by Peter Wight, Frank Lee and Harold Gimblett. I am not a facts and figures man but there were plenty of people around me to tell me when I broke all those records. I couldn't tell them about the pills, of course, but in the eyes of the public I was very much the man of the hour and they rewarded me with that fine benefit cheque. To cap a magnificent year I was honoured when the cricket bible, "Wisden", named me as one of their five players of the year. All five recipients were Australians. Richie Benaud, Alan Davidson, Norman O'Neill and Bill Lawry were the other four, having earned their mention by playing big parts in the Ashes victory over England. The thought used to occur to me in an idle moment that if Benaud's tourists had some injuries they might be forced to call me up as replacement. I laughed about it then, as a 42 year old, but they would have been hard-pressed to find an Australian in better form that summer.

My only regret about my finest season was that I did not take more wickets. Harold Stephenson was the Somerset captain by now and I think he made the error of not giving me more bowling. I should not complain about a haul of 62 wickets at an average of 25.33, but I felt I should have been closer to the 100 mark. He believed I was getting so many runs that to over-bowl me would be a mistake. In previous seasons I had thrived on work and my apprenticeship in the Lancashire leagues had prepared me to be involved in the game at all times. But very often he would take me off just when I had begun to work up a sweat. He must have reasoned that, at my age, I could not do both, and all the while I was scoring runs by the bucketful, he used me sparingly as a bowler. I suppose I should have been satisfied with my record-breaking achievement with the bat, but it still rankles slightly to this day that I was not allowed the chance to do the 3,000 runs and 100 wickets double.

Just before the start of the next season I decided to have a little wager. I am not a betting man by nature. I saw my father fritter away too much money ever to be tempted to make it a regular habit, but this was different. I marched into a bookies in Taunton and said: "What price will you give me to do the 1,000 runs and 100 wicket double this season?" I pointed out to him that I was now 43 and that although 1,000 runs was well within my scope I had never before taken 100 wickets in an English county season. The bookie thought about it. Surely old Bill couldn't keep it up much longer.

Standing the Test of Time

"All right," he said, "Ten to one is the price. Take it or leave it." No sooner had he said it than I slapped £50 on his desk. He raised his eyebrows; the bet was on. I may not have had the doctor's mystery pills to help me but I needed no greater incentive.

For five months I concentrated like I have never concentrated before. And, the day after stumps had been drawn for the last time in September, I made my way back to that bookies having scored 1915 runs and taken the little matter of 112 wickets. "You owe me £500," I said with a smirk of triumph. "Lucky bugger!" he replied as he counted out my winnings in five pound notes. As I downed a couple of pints in celebration, I reflected on his statement. A bugger I might have been; lucky I was not.

On the contrary, I had earned my winnings. I might not have batted quite so well as in the previous year, but three centuries and an average of 36.82 reflected my steadiness, and it is a source of regret that I was not able to manage the extra 85 runs which would have made me the first Somerset player to have scored 2,000 runs and taken 100 wickets in a season. I persuaded Stephenson to give me more bowling and I repaid his faith by performing better than ever with the ball. I never doubted my ability to take 100 wickets and on six occasions I took five or more in an innings. My final haul of 112 wickets cost me just 20.74 each. In one incredible match against Leicestershire at Ashby-de-la-Zouch I took nine in the match for 95 runs, scored 44 and 26 not out, including the winning hit, and did a little stint as substitute wicketkeeper. As I reminded Stephenson afterwards, the more I was involved the better I played. In all, it was another great season and it was recognised by my fellow professionals around the counties when they voted me "Cricketer of the Year". Of the 162 votes cast by capped players, 72 of them were for me. Any award is pleasant, but when it comes from other players, it is all the sweeter.

I often wonder how it was that a player of my age should take such an honour ahead of so many younger men, but even at that stage I had noticed that standards within the English game were beginning to deteriorate. Many people think it is only in recent years that it has declined to its present low ebb. I feel it was starting to happen way back in the early sixties. Somerset were improving as a team because the outdated preference for amateurs had died - but other counties were weakening. Surrey fell from grace, never being able to replace the big names, and Yorkshire began a slide which they have never been able to halt. We narrowed the gap to the extent that we no longer went into matches expecting and receiving inevitable defeat. While I was pleased more counties were becoming involved in the destination of the big prizes, the major universities were no longer unearthing people like Cowdrey and May and the suffering began. Having played and umpired in English first class cricket for 28 years, I think I can pinpoint the start of the present troubles to the time when, oddly enough, I was at my peak. Now there is precious little genuine quality around anywhere in the world - and I can assure you that is not the soured opinion of an old man but the considered thoughts of someone who has spent a lifetime in cricket.

5
The 1960's

AUSTRALIAN CRICKETERS HAVE built up an unenviable record for "sledging", as they call it, over the years. I reckon I must have done a bit of it myself when I lived there, but I was on the receiving end in 1961 when Benaud brought his touring party to Taunton for the match against us.

"Sledging" is Aussie slang for trying to unsettle your opponent by giving him some lip as he tries to concentrate. It is usually punctuated by a series of four-letter words, and for batsmen with brittle temperaments it can be very distressing. Don't get me wrong, the Aussies do not have a monopoly on this crease-side chit-chat, but they are better at it than everyone else. As an umpire at Test level it was something I never fully came to terms with. As a player, it shocked even me. It was the year I scored a lot of runs against the tourists, both for Somerset and Arthur Gilligans' XI in a representative match at Hastings towards the end of the summer. The Aussies wanted to get me out, partly because that year I was obviously the danger man but also, I suspect, because the old wounds about deserters had still not fully healed. Before I had got off the mark I played at a delivery from Gaunt and, I believe to this day, never got a touch. But Barry Jarman, the wicketkeeper, was equally positive I had and, with his slip fielders, yelled for the catch.

Now, as a batsman, I always walked if I thought I was out. It was a habit that was drilled in as a youngster and was something I carried on doing until the day I retired. These days, it is different again. You have to carry them off the field before they leave the crease. But in this instance I was sure there was no question of me being out so I stayed rooted to the spot. Johnny Arnold, the umpire, was unmoved. "Not out", he said, and I prepared myself for the next ball. The Aussies went mad. I was called every name under the sun, of which "cheat" is the only one I can repeat here. Their attitude surprised and then angered me. So I got my head down and grafted my way to one of the most satisfying centuries of my life.

When I reached my ton, the crowded little ground at Taunton erupted in hysterical delight. If Benaud put his hands together to applaud, then he was the only Australian who did so. They were convinced I was out 100 runs ago and the sarcastic carping continued even then. Had they been slightly more forgiving I might have been tempted to get myself out, but instead I got my head down once more and went on to make 134 very satisfying runs.

My relationship with the Australians in that particular match had collapsed completely and the mood was decidedly hostile when I took guard for the second innings. Once more, I was determined not to get out cheaply, if only because I wanted to grind Jarman and his cackling cronies into the ground. At 95 I was on the threshold of my second century of the match – news of which was sure to cause a stir or two back in Sydney. Then Gaunt bowled me. As I trooped back to the pavilion to a standing ovation from the spectators, Jarman started again. "You sure you're out?" he inquired as he surveyed the wreckage of my wicket. "Give him the benefit of the doubt," he shouted aloud, but out of Arnold's earshot. He could say what he liked. The runs were in the book and I'm only sorry I was five runs short of a memorable achievement.

Curiously, and sadly, the incident lingered when I returned to Australia in 1976 on an all-expenses paid trip to appear on a "This Is Your Life" programme. Someone I had never even met mentioned the catch-that-never-was and asked: "Why didn't you walk?". I told him for one very good reason. I was not out and the umpire had agreed with me. Even so, it was disturbing to think that 15 years on the subject of one little controversy was still in the minds of people who had not even seen it. What did the Australian sports reporters write and say about me? I can only think they made me out to be the villain.

Later in the summer I was selected to play against an England XI for a Commonwealth XI at Hastings and I travelled down to the Sussex resort still needing about 130 runs for my 3,000. By that stage of the season it had become important to me to reach that target. I took my time in the first innings and made 102. This left me an insubstantial number to get second time around, and in due course I got them.

I am not saying I was the innocent victim in all these clashes through my career. I always gave as good as I got, particularly against other renowned hard men. And they didn't come much harder or more durable than Brian Close. Close was a crazy man at times and I laugh now when I remember one or two of our little squabbles. We were playing Yorkshire at Bath in 1959 and doing rather well against them, I recall. I must have been getting a few wickets because when Close came in he decided to unsettle and disturb my rhythm. As I was coming in to bowl, Close started to advance, his bat held high behind him like he was going to attempt to hit me out of the ground. There was nothing wrong with that, except that he was deliberately spiking the wicket on or around a length. I could see what he was doing but the umpire could not. I pointed it out to him. I said: "Look what he is doing to the wicket". The umpire could not believe the evidence of his own eyes. "Play on", he said. I was furious and I took the law into my own hands. I told Close: "If you don't stop doing that, I'll give you a beamer". Close acted as the aggrieved party. "What am I doing wrong?" he pleaded innocently. Sort of walking off in disgust, I decided there was only one way to make my protest. I sat down in the crease at the other end and refused to bowl. For several minutes play came to a standstill as I refused to continue unless Close was prevented from carrying out his evil scheme. The umpire told me he was doing nothing illegal. I was told to play on or go off the field. Close had won the day. "Ready when you are Bill", he said as I went back to my mark. I might have lost the battle but I didn't lose the war. I am pleased to say Somerset overcame Close et al to win the match. Honour was satisfied.

Butch White, the Hampshire fast bowler, was another one with whom I always had a battle or two. Butch was decidedly quick when he wanted to be and was good enough to get a cap or two for

England when he was in his prime. As a left-handed batsman, coming in down the order, he could also hit the ball very hard and very high. One day the mood took him to have a go at me. My first three deliveries were lifted over the ropes for sixes. I could see he had made up his mind to put the next three the same way. "You bastard," I told him, "I bet you don't hit the other three". Butch could be a tough customer but he laughed. I was puzzled and not a little worried. What was he planning? I need not have been concerned. My next three balls were met with textbook forward defensive strokes. "I can defend as well, Bill", he shouted back.

Malcolm Nash of Glamorgan had the misfortune to be the first person to enter the record books for having conceded 36 in an over in a first-class match. Gary Sobers dispatched him for six successive sixes at Swansea and poor Malcolm never lived it down. He will always be remembered for that one over, which is a shame because in certain conditions he was not a bad county player and a great servant to Glamorgan for over 18 years. One day while I was umpiring, there was a lull in play and I got talking to Malcolm. I told him I could not understand how he let himself be hit around like that by Sobers. Surely a bowler of his quality ought to have been able to bowl something even Sobers could not have struck for six. It was obviously a question he had been asked many times before and he will have to answer it many times again, I am sure. "Bill," he said, "I honestly believed I could get him out every ball. That is why I attacked. If I thought he was going to hit me for six sixes I would have been more defensive, but I was buying his wicket and it didn't work". I found it impossible to feel anything but pity for Malcolm, living proof that attacking is not always the best strategy in sport.

Somerset's own gradual rise in prominence during the 1960s was in no small measure due to the recruitment of the giant figure of Fred Rumsey. Fred, if my memory does not play tricks, must have been 6 ft 5 ins and big with it. I am sure he will take it the right way when I describe him as an awkward, unathletic sort of character, but in his case looks were deceptive. He added a whole new dimension to our cricket because, for the first time since I had been at Taunton, we had taken on a genuinely fast bowler. I must admit a few eyebrows were raised when he showed up for pre-season training and was introduced to us as the man who could give it to 'em back. After all, his pedigree hardly suggested that other counties would be quaking in their boots when confronted by our new signing. Born in London, he had spent three largely unproductive years at Worcestershire, who had not shown any interest in retaining him any longer. When Somerset brought him west, he was 27 years old – hardly in the first flush of youth – with a very mediocre record behind him. But the county had a habit of finding a little bit of gold amongst other people's rubbish, and in the case of Fred Rumsey, he soon became worth his considerable weight in any precious metal.

He may not have looked much like a sportsman but Fred quickly won us over with his boundless enthusiasm and his willingness to work. But his greatest assets were his speed and bounce. I am not saying he was the fastest bowler in the country all of the time he was in action, but he could be very fast in short spells with his left-arm delivery and he soon became another folk-hero. Almost immediately, other, better equipped counties started to dish out less of the short-pitched stuff at us. They talk about the excess nowadays of the bouncer but, believe me, as a county who did not have the fire power to hit back, we got more than our share of deliveries specifically aimed to intimidate us. Suddenly Fred came from nowhere and began to give others a taste of their own, unpalatable medicine and for several pleasant years we were treated with respect.

Mind you, Fred had to be wound up to have a go at anyone. He was the proverbial gentle giant who did not like hurting, or even scaring, opponents unnecessarily. I used to say: "Go on Fred, give the batsman a bouncer." Time after time he refused to do so. "I might kill somebody", he would reply. That sort of thing needled me. For five or six years I had been ducking and weaving from one end of England to the other and, now that we had a potent weapon of our own, damned if I wasn't going to get the best out of him.

Sure enough, after a few overs of me stirring him up, he would unleash a really hostile bouncer just when the batsman looked set, and the fear and panic this induced brought a contented smile to my gnarled old features.

I am pleased to report that Fred was instantly successful. He made his debut for us in 1963 and, like me, was capped in his first season. A year later he was in the Test team against Australia at Old Trafford and, although he missed out on the tour Down Under the following winter, still did enough in county cricket to earn another three caps against New Zealand in the summer of 1965 and a fifth facing the South Africans during the same season. He might not have been a Test class player but he never let England down and, at the time, with so many good bowlers from which to choose, Fred earned the right to his England opportunities. He took a total of 102 wickets in 1963 and 119 in 1965 at an average of 16.18, figures which speak eloquently for themselves. I believe his signing was the turning point for Somerset and, while he did not last many years, he did a fair amount of damage when he chose to do so and I, for one, was immensely glad to see it. When Fred forgot his inhibitions and the gentle side of his nature, he could bowl as fast as anyone in the country and there was not a batsman around the counties who did not treat him with caution and, on some notable occasions, a little fear as well.

I like to think I played my part in getting Fred the first of his England caps. One day, Alec Bedser came up and asked about him as his acting captain. Fred might have been a power at domestic level but how would he rate against top class players in the Test arena? I was surprised the England selectors were interested in him. Somerset players had not exactly filled the England teams of recent years and, to be fair, we had not been over-endowed with players of international potential while I had been a Somerset cricketer. He obviously did not know much about Fred except that he was big, great-hearted and picking up wickets left, right and centre for Somerset. He came down to run the rule over Fred in one county match and was still not sure what to make of this shambling character who could not bat to save his life and who did not move around the field with, how shall I put it, the grace of a gazelle!

But I soon put Bedser's mind at rest. I told him: "Use him in short bursts and he is as quick and as lively as anyone you care to name". In short, I said Fred was very much a strike bowler who, handled properly, could take care of himself against the best. England took a chance and in late July 1964, Fred was called up to face Bobby Simpson's men, who were already one up after three matches. He took the wickets of Tom Veivers and Wally Grout but his two for 99 was not enough to earn him a second game that summer. Even so, Fred was as happy as a child in a playground when he got his cap and he was the first to thank me for my efforts on his behalf.

Fred was as an unusual bloke off the field as he was on it. He was the team's number one socialiser in all its different forms. The rest of the Somerset team were primarily beer drinkers. But not Fred. He fancied himself as a bit of a wine expert and, while his teammates would be grateful for anything to quench their thirsts after a hard day in the field, Fred would like nothing better than to taste a glass of wine for quality, delicately swilling little mouthfuls around in his chops before complaining in a loud voice it was not chilled enough for his liking. At least he made us laugh. One of his favourite tricks was to get to the bar first and say: "What are you having?" to all and sundry. Having committed himself to an exceptionally large round he would quietly slope away to the toilets until someone else, namely me as often as not, had been forced to pick up the bill. Then he would stroll back in and look absolutely astounded when told that his round had been paid for him in his absence. This happened many times and yet he always got away with it. There was a certain charm about him and, because he never let us down in the field, we were prepared to overlook his misdemeanours in the bar. Fred may have kept us amused with his insistence that "I'll pay the next round", and his constant disputes with waiters over the size of bills, but when it came to cricket he was deadly serious and played a big part in what success we achieved in the mid 1960s.

The Gillette Cup was introduced in 1963 and it revolutionised an ailing game. Cricket had been crying out for the thrills of instant, same-day results and the new competition was welcomed with open arms by the majority of players and the vast majority of the game's dwindling public. It often occurs to me what might have happened had the new cup not been brought in. The three-day county championship was dying on its feet and I suppose it might not have been long before one or more counties simply went out of business. With people like Botham and Viv Richards at their disposal, Somerset built a tradition for excellence in the cup competitions in the 1980's, but I feel sure we laid the foundations for their subsequent glories by tackling the demands of the new Gillette Cup rather more enthusiastically and scientifically than many of our rivals.

In 1963 we were knocked out in the first round by Glamorgan, but in 1966 fell at the last hurdle, beaten in the semi-final. It was on our way to the semi-final that we disposed of Ted Dexter's Sussex who, at that stage of the competition, were its acknowledged masters. I scored 38 not out and then took four wickets, including Dexter and Jim Parks, for just 14. This performance was enough to earn me the coveted man-of-the-match award, and, as a team, it gave us the confidence to realise we were capable of reaching the final at Lord's. The following summer this is precisely what we did.

Our run to the final began with a comfortable 91-run win over Leicestershire, with Graham Burgess top-scoring with 73. Our next opponents were the holders, Warwickshire, on their own ground at Edgbaston. My personal contribution of 45 runs and three wickets for 24 helped us gain a victory in a rain-affected match by 25 runs and earned me my second man-of-the-match medal. It was a great win for us and we all began to feel that 1967 could well be our year. I was man of the match in the next round with 30 and two for eight off twelve overs against Northamptonshire. Fred Rumsey struck a crucial blow for us when he had the prolific and devastating England opener Colin Milburn out with his second delivery. Once more we batted and bowled tightly to earn a semi-final place against Lancashire at Old Trafford. No one in their right mind would wish to play a match as important as the semi-final at a place like Old Trafford and we hardly relished the prospect. But we not only won the match and booked a place at Lord's, we slaughtered poor old Lancashire, and match adjudicator Herbert Sutcliffe, a Yorkshireman naturally, was absolutely correct when he described the Lancashire reply to our modest 211 as a "debacle". We beat them by 100 runs and the big crowd at Old Trafford was numbed into silence as the home team's wickets tumbled in rapid succession after Barry Wood and the former Somerset opener Graham Atkinson had put on 40 for the first wicket.

So suddenly I was on my way to a Lord's final at 48 years of age, the oldest player in county cricket. By now I had long ceased to be surprised by the twists and turns of my extraordinary career, but even I was shocked by the response of the Somerset public to the biggest occasion in the club's history. Our secretary, Richard Robinson, estimated he could have sold the club's allocation of 5,250 tickets three times over, and exiled supporters from all over the world made a point of being at Lord's to see us take on Colin Cowdrey's talented Kent side that early September Saturday. Our route to the ground was lined that day with Somerset fans draped in smocks, covered in straw and knocking back the county's own special brew, cider. Inside the famous old arena they out-shouted and overwhelmed the more straight-laced Kent followers, some of whom made it clear in no uncertain terms that cricket was a game to be enjoyed in silence.

I only wish the story had a happy ending - but we lost by 32 runs when we should have won, and I can, even now, admit to one or two pangs of regret at letting down our noisy band of admirers. It was a low-scoring game and looking at the details again, a feeling of irritation returns because we really should have been able to overhaul Kent's disappointing score of 193. Mike Denness, who later went on to lead England, and Brian Luckhurst gave them a bright start with 78 in 19 overs for the first wicket, but then I took a hand. I had Denness caught at the wicket, but at lunch Kent were in the powerful position of 129 for one with the awesome Cowdrey still to come. Later I struck to get rid of Luckhurst for 54 in a spell of two for three in four overs, and Kent began to slide. Cowdrey was caught at midwicket for one and his side never recovered. From 138 for one, they lost their last nine wickets for 55 runs and I ended with three for 22 from my allocation of 12 overs. With a target of only just over three an over there was a mood of optimism and expectation in the Somerset dressing room before we began our reply.

Roy Virgin and Peter Robinson whittled down the requirement with a stand of 58 for the first wicket, but they put pressure on us by taking so long to score their runs, 17 overs for the first 51 runs. Our optimism turned to annoyance as they took their time at a crucial stage in the match. Now Roy is still a good friend of mine and at the height of his career with Somerset and later Northamptonshire he was a consistently heavy run scorer who might even have played for England had he played for a more fashionable pair of counties. But when he came back after plodding away for 17 I gave him a piece of my mind, accusing him of making it tough for the rest of us by taking too long to get going and then getting out at a time when he should have been looking to accelerate. I felt he had been playing for himself and not the team and I told him so. I was not exactly in the best of moods when I came out to bat at number five to a tumultuous reception from both Somerset and Kent supporters.

We were 84 for three and the overs were fast running out. I realised so much depended on me and at my age it was asking a lot to scamper quick singles to take away the initiative from the Kent bowlers. I managed only eight before I was superbly caught at backward short leg by Alan Brown off John Shepherd, the West Indian, and in spite of some brave hitting by Graham Burgess we quietly fell away to defeat while our supporters had only the consolation of their cider to nurse them through the anti-climax.

Standing the Test of Time

Kent showed the steadier nerve on the day and that night I was out celebrating a smashing occasion, even if it was the last great event of my playing career.

To play at Lord's is always special; to do so in the cup final will remain one of the great moments of my life. Our fans did not hold it against us for long. They sang and danced and drank all the way back to Taunton and the wonderful countryside of Somerset. They had been part of an outstanding day and they were determined to repeat it. Thanks to Botham and Richards and other fine players there, they have been able to return to Lord's many times since. My only regret is that I don't have a winner's medal in my trophy cabinet. That would have been the seal on my life in cricket.

If the 1967 season ended on a pleasant and happy note, the mood a year later, for me at least, was contrastingly sour. It had not been a particularly good summer for any of us, but even at the age of 49 I still managed to score 1219 runs and take 36 wickets. I reckoned I was fit and strong enough to continue for several more years but, I'm afraid, Somerset did not. I received a letter from them which hurts even now as I look at it. Dated 11th September, it reads: "Dear Bill, At the committee meeting today it was decided to offer you terms for Sunday League and Gillette Cup matches in 1969. Perhaps you would be good enough to call at my office so that I may discuss the details with you." It was signed Richard Robinson, the secretary.

I was absolutely staggered. I had never been sacked before and this was definitely a letter of goodbye. The Sunday League was about to be introduced for 1969 and it provided a maximum of 16 matches. Only one match could, of course, be guaranteed in the Gillette Cup. From a quick, on-the-spot calculation I worked out I could only earn about £300 the following season and, with two sons still at school, it was just not on. I had reached the end of the line and I was very upset. Indeed, I was still reeling from the shock of the letter when the phone started ringing. It was the first of several calls from the Press. They had obviously found out in advance and, for the first time in my life, I was lost for an explanation. How they

58

found out I shall never know, but my own feelings of stunned disappointment were worsened by the knowledge that the Press knew about my dismissal before I did.

I couldn't understand how Somerset could treat me like this. I had been with them eleven years and there had not been the slightest hint I would not be getting another contract. In fact, I was beginning to think in terms of a testimonial, so confident was I of continuing. In all my years with Somerset I had missed only about three games and had been a permanent fixture in the team – much as I had been from the moment I had arrived. I had put a lot of myself into cricket, and Somerset in particular, touring the far-flung corners of the county in the winters to deliver by my estimation over 300 after-dinner speeches on the club's behalf. Now they were just throwing me out, without so much as a thank-you. When I recovered my senses I went into Taunton to see Robinson. He told me they were looking to the future and they were going to introduce some youngsters. I could hardly argue with him on that score but I felt age was immaterial. I told him I would be prepared to continue playing three-day matches on a non-contract basis. They could pay me by the match and only when they needed me.

I wanted to stay in cricket and while Somerset promised to consider my counter-proposal, I applied to join the list of first class umpires. The powers at Lord's were pleased to receive my application, but I think, even at that stage, I would have liked to have carried on playing if at all possible. Somerset kept delaying and delaying. Every time the subject was due to be discussed, the meeting never took place because someone could not get there. The deadline for a final application for the umpires' list was the end of September. By the time that date came, I had still not received any reply from the county. Lord's agreed to extend their deadline while I waited. Then, eventually it came. Somerset were prepared to stand by their original offer but they did not want me for championship matches. I rang Lord's immediately. Career number four was about to begin.

Standing the Test of Time

It was a sad and unhappy way to end a mutually beneficial relationship. Somerset had been revitalised while I had been a playing member and I like to think I had played my part. I could have understood it a little more easily if they had started to bring in younger players. Instead, in the next year or two they recruited from other counties Tom Cartwright, Jim Parks and Brian Close, none of whom could have been described as "youngsters", even by their mothers! Unfortunately, I do not think my relationship with the county has ever been properly repaired, much as I still love the club and the area. After I became an umpire I was never invited to have a free drink or meal with the committee. To them I was just another umpire. That was until the new clubhouse was opened at the Taunton ground. Herbie Hoskins told Betty and me to come and have a drink after play one day. I was delighted after all this time to accept. But when I got there, no one bought me a drink. I had to get my own and, just to make matters worse, when several prominent members of the committee saw me at the bar they thrust their glasses forward for me to replenish them. I have never been so insulted in my life. Betty and I downed our drinks and left without another word.

I was deeply sorry and saddened by the way my playing career ended. Over the years I have been equally hurt that the damage has not been properly repaired. When I retired from umpiring, the club had the decency to present me with a decanter and a set of glasses. For that, I thank them. But I wonder if they would have done so had David Shepherd, a fellow umpire, not pointedly said to the chairman one day during my last season: "What are you going to give Bill when he retires?".

60

6
Captaincy

ONE OF THE BIGGEST disappointments of my career was that I was never given an extended opportunity as captain. As a professional in the Lancashire leagues, my job was to advise an amateur skipper. I accepted this and it did not bother me because I had more than enough to worry about as principal batsman and principal bowler. Maurice Tremlett was the captain at Somerset when I first arrived and it was a privilege to serve under him. When he moved on, my mate Harold Stephenson took over and he did a thoroughly competent job until he injured his back during the 1964 season. I was flattered and delighted when I was called aside when it became obvious Stephenson was going to be out of action for a long spell and asked to take over until he was able to return. I was pleased because every player would like a shot at the job at some time in their career and I was certainly no exception. I was then 45 and had been playing cricket more years than I cared to remember, but I felt I was well qualified and for the rest of the summer carried it out to the best of my ability.

Stephenson played in only three matches that year and retired at the end of it, leaving a vacancy for the following year. Since I had been captain for the other 26 matches, I naturally assumed I would be given the captaincy on a permanent basis in 1965. Somerset had finished in eighth position and the players were happy to take orders from me. One or two committee men had even intimated privately that I had done enough to satisfy everyone and it would all be a formality when the time came to make a decision. Imagine my surprise – horror is probably a better word – when it was announced that Colin Atkinson, an amateur with far less first-class experience, would be leading Somerset in 1965. It was a hell of a shock. I was not the only seasoned professional to have his nose put out of joint. Most of the others expressed similar disquiet. Even the club's followers were surprised and a little disappointed. After all, this 33 year old Millfield teacher from the North East was not as well known as me. People stopped me in the Taunton streets. "Why aren't you skipper Bill?" they asked. I only wish I had an answer for them because it was difficult to conceal my annoyance and hurt. But I was under contract and there was no alternative but to soldier on under Mr. C.R.M Atkinson, amateur captain and new leader of Somerset County Cricket Club.

Somerset, like many rural counties, had always gone for an amateur captain and Tremlett was the first professional skipper. When Stephenson replaced him I thought the days of amateur leaders were over at last and, in my estimation, not before time. But suddenly the clock was turned back and in stepped Atkinson with the difficult job of persuading a doubting playing staff that he was up to the task. His background did not suggest he was. He had played only two matches for the county in 1963 and none at all in 1964. What is more, I was not alone in being unconvinced that he was a good enough player in his own right to lead us from the front.

Colin Atkinson was not a great player, he will be the first to admit. But in fairness to him he gradually won us over. I was sceptical and probably a little unhelpful when he started, and he would have been pretty insensitive not to have noticed my resentment. By sheer strength of character and hard work he was determined to overcome our apprehensions, and he did. Batting at number six, he grafted away in a bid to make light of a restriction caused by arthritis and in one season he succeeded in scoring 1,000 runs. In many ways it was unfair of the club to make him captain above me and others perhaps better qualified, but he earned our respect and although he was never the greatest player to represent Somerset, I came to like him.

Not that he thought so. When the time came for him to resume his academic career at Millfield, we had a farewell dinner. He rose to his feet and in the course of his speech, he said: "There is one

man here not sorry to see me go. And that's Bill Alley.".". It was all
a bit embarrassing, more particularly because by that stage it was
not true. Sure enough, I hardly went out of my way to help him
when he first took over but by the end it was different. He had
shown us that by guts, hard work and a genuine approach that he
was taking his cricket seriously, and, for all his failings, he had my
support. Since then, I am pleased to say, we have become good
friends, but I don't think I ever fully convinced him that I was on
his side. Even so, my chances of being captain had gone forever
and I resigned myself to being one of the led rather than a leader
for the rest of my playing career.

Captaincy is an art and in my time the most impressive exponent
has been Mike Brearley, without any shadow of a doubt. Much has
been said about the man; the way he hummed classical music to
himself while he batted; his love for the finer things in life, and his
intellectual interest in philosophy. All this may give the impression
of him as a fusty academic playing cricket as a relaxation, or even
to further his studies into the human condition. Nothing could be
further from the truth. He was a hard and calculating leader who
got the best out of his players and knew how to win. Don't let his
rather aloof attitude fool anyone. Here was a man dedicated to
beating his opponent, and his record with England and Middlesex
showed he did not fail very often.

As an umpire it was easy to see who were the captains who
knew what they were doing. Brearley was the only skipper in my
time on the umpires' list who never panicked – at international or
domestic level. On the field he never said much to anyone and yet
he was in total command. Those who played under him always
made a point of saying how fair he was. If he was obliged to
reprimand any errant player, he did so in the quiet of the dressing-
room, never in front of the gallery and he was universally respected
for his ability to cajole, push and pull his teams through any crisis.
Even when he was under the greatest pressure, he consistently gave
the impression he had plenty of time to make his decisions. He
would joke, smile and even laugh just when, to any observer in the

midst of the action, he could have been forgiven for turning into a gibbering wreck, as some of his contemporaries did.

I am told that he was quite capable of delivering a broadside if the occasion demanded and, in his time with both Middlesex and England, there were some awkward customers who needed the occasional kick up the backside. At Middlesex he had a very powerful county team at his disposal, laced with Test players or with players of near international class. When they were at full-strength, Middlesex were a powerful unit, made all the more formidable by Brearley's shrewd and inspiring captaincy. The pressure was off him at Middlesex because of the standard of player he had working for him, but even when he led England - and he struggled in his own right as a player to bridge the big gap between county and Test cricket - he was still very much the boss and always seemingly in control of his own destiny. Above all, he was a master tactician, his cool, unruffled exterior concealing a sharp brain which was always working for the good of the team.

It was much harder for Brearley when he took over the England team. The Kerry Packer affair had blown the game apart and his predecessor Tony Greig had helped detonate the explosion. Several key members of the England team had defected to Packer and his World Series circus and players like Derek Underwood, Alan Knott and even Greig himself were not easily replaced. But Brearley succeeded in uniting all factions, getting the best out of what talent was left at his command and winning matches. Sometimes I don't think he got the credit he deserved. Even when he went to Australia in 1978-9 and won the Ashes series by five matches to one, he was hailed as "lucky". I agree he was fortunate to come across an Australian side shorn of nearly all the big names, but England were also missing some and the Tests still had to be won - on Australian wickets. It might have been different if both teams had been at full strength, but the simple fact of the matter was that they were not and Brearley won hands down because he outwitted Graham Yallop with a fair amount of ease.

Captaincy

Now I am not going to accuse him of gamesmanship but Brearley knew how to look after himself on the field and, as an umpire, I was involved in an interesting little incident with him when Middlesex were playing Sussex at Lord's on an overcast morning when Imran Khan was at his magnificent best and was making one of his periodic returns from injury, bowling as fast as I have ever seen him. The sheer pace of his deliveries would have been enough to occupy the attentions of the very best, but in the conditions he was also swinging the ball violently. Quite honestly, I don't think "Brears" had a clue what to do. He must have played and missed five times out of every six he faced from the great Pakistani. How he survived that first half an hour I will never know – and nor will poor old Imran, who could scarcely believe his ill-fortune as Brearley pushed and prodded without so much as laying bat to ball. It was embarrassing to watch as Brearley's discomfort was as plain to see as Imran's mounting anger. This state of affairs could not go on much longer and both parties knew it. Something had to happen and, if the Middlesex skipper was to last much longer, he had to do something about it. And he did.

Brearley suddenly called a halt to the proceedings and, picking up the ball, brought it to me. "What do you make of this?" he said, inviting me to examine it. I could see absolutely nothing wrong with the ball which, after all, was only a few overs old, however unpleasant they may have been for him. Brearley had nevertheless sowed the seeds of doubt in my mind. Was he trying to tell me Imran was picking the seam? A few deliveries later, Brearley again asked me to look at the ball. I called over the other umpire. Neither of us saw anything remotely amiss. "Play on" I said. Soon afterwards, Brearley was out and it was only later that I realised what he had been up to. He had wanted us to change the ball because he felt there either had to be some defect which made it swing as much as it did, or Imran was doing something illegal to the seam. I am not accusing him of attempting to "con" me. He was just trying to make a point, and very craftily he did it. Anyway, he chose the wrong man to fool over seam-picking. I had done it as a player for

Standing the Test of Time

30 years and if Imran was guilty, he certainly had not made a very good job of it.

That aside, Brearley is the best for me. I was a great fan of Phil Edmonds, the left arm spin bowler and a member of Brearley's teams at Middlesex and England. I liked the man but he got extremely worked up on the field and it is no secret that he has caused Brearley some problems. I think Edmonds is a perfectionist and a strong individual and he is not scared to vent his feelings. For all that, Brearley handled him magnificently and got the best out of his considerable talent, channelling his skills to the benefit of the team and never once while I was an umpire, clashing with him on the field. It was Brearley also who turned the big West Indian fast bowler Wayne Daniel into a match-winner when he first came over from Barbados. Wayne was a large, muscle-bound boy who can be fast and hostile when he chooses. Brearley realised his qualities and used him in short and sharp bursts. For his first few years at Middlesex, under Brearley's control, he was the most feared bowler in county cricket. Curiously, he was never the same threat when playing for the West Indies. Admittedly, they have many similar bowlers but, and no disrespect to Clive Lloyd here, Brearley knew how to use him properly and for a short time at least he turned him from raw newcomer into a very potent weapon.

Brearley, in the eyes of all concerned in the game, will go down as one of the most outstanding leaders of his time, certainly while I was an umpire. In his manner, his field-placing, his handling of bowlers and his ability to keep control of a match, he was without peer. He was the sole boss on the field, and that cannot be said about every captain, and he was pleasant with it. Fair, modest and thoroughly ruthless.

When I first came into the first-class game, Don Bradman was not only Australia's top batsman and the best in the world indisputably, he was also captain of his adopted state, South Australia and his country. His leadership was never questioned. He had only to crack his fingers and the team stood to attention. A withering look delivered from a couple of hundred yards could ruin a hard man's day. He had no need to raise his voice or even speak at all. To play for Bradman required complete dedication and discipline, and he got it. He made it clear that to play for Australia was a privilege few had the pleasure of enjoying. There could be no higher honour for an Australian than to wear the green and gold cap, and it had to be earned. I believe some of his teammates might even have been a little in awe of him because there was always an instant response to any of his orders. He set standards of leadership for Australia which others have been fortunate enough to inherit. By demanding complete obedience, Bradman was able to get on with the job of batting, which he did better than anyone else in his era, and those under him to get on with their own personal tasks. As a result, those teams Bradman led were strong individually, but also very much a unit. The Australian squad of 1948 which came to England is a classic example.

Richie Benaud is one of the captains who was able to take advantage of the mode of discipline created by Bradman's no-nonsense approach. I liked Richie from the moment I first clapped eyes on him in his pram at Petersham. He wasn't playing in those days, of course, but his father was and I have watched his career develop with interest. He followed in a great line of Australian captains, and he by no means paled in comparison. He is a pleasant man, both on and off the field, but like Bradman, completely in control – as I discovered when I played against his 1961 tourists at Taunton.

Benaud's team that year has not always been applauded as much as it should have been, and I am not just saying that because of all the runs I scored against his tourists. His success in England was the culmination of several years of careful planning and the moulding of some fine young talent into a potent force. Richie obviously thought it hard to follow an Ashes victory on foreign soil and retired at a time when he might well have carried on for a few more years and earned his rightful place among the great all-rounders by weight of runs and wickets. Like Brearley, he was a cool and calculating skipper who never let a fraught situation get to him. The same could not be said for Brian Close.

Standing the Test of Time

Poor old Closey. He will think I have got it in for him. I can assure you this is simply not true, but things always seemed to happen to Brian when I was around. The old Yorkshire war-horse was a talented cricketer, but when it came to captaincy and the leadership of men, Brian got rattled very easily. He struck me as a panicky sort of character on the field. I well remember, for instance, being in charge of a vital John Player League match at Cardiff where Glamorgan were playing Somerset, for whom Close was by then skipper. It must have been near the end of the 1976 season and two or three teams were in with a chance of winning the title that Sunday, including Somerset. My old county had started the day as favourites, if only because Glamorgan did not represent the hardest of final hurdles.

In those days the Sunday League was televised regularly, with one featured match shown it its entirety on BBC 2. The television guys made a habit when the title was close to being decided of hiring a helicopter and dropping on the new champions to present them with the trophy within minutes of the final ball being bowled. It was a good idea and made for extra drama. Somerset panicked after Close had gone for one and Botham for nine, and requiring three off the last ball, Burgess could score only two as Colin Dredge was run out by inches going for a third. Closey lost his way that time, and if he's honest, as I know he is, he'll admit he threw it away. The helicopter headed instead for Maidstone.

One of the captains for whom I had the highest regard was the Yorkshireman, Ray Illingworth, who achieved so much when he led both Leicestershire and England. Some Yorkshiremen have a thoroughly deserved reputation for being dour and defensive, but Ray was always pleasantly positive. He wanted to win and was prepared to take chances to bring about victory. For instance, he would have no hesitation in using his spin bowlers from the first over of an innings if he thought by doing so he could win a match, and I do not remember many others who did that. His greatest strength was the way he handled his bowlers, always spotting weaknesses in the batsmen that could be exploited and calling up the right men at the right time to cash in. It was an education to watch him at work and I greatly admired his professionalism.

Mind you, he did have his quirks. Ray seemed to me the sort of guy who always had to have everything absolutely in the correct order. He was a perfectionist who, quite rightly in my view, was not prepared to accept any half measures. There was a time when I had a potentially nasty little problem on my hands the day Ray brought his Leicestershire team down to Bournemouth to take on Hampshire. Dean Park is a pretty little ground and is not usually the centre of any great controversies. The groundsman, in his wisdom, had marked out a wicket on the far edge of the square making one boundary very much shorter than the other. While it was noticeably lop-sided, I was prepared to overlook it. After all, the conditions were the same for both sides. But not Ray. He was hopping mad. How dare they ruin the game by putting the wicket in the wrong place, he fumed. He told me there was only one way around this mess. I was to order that the president's tent and a little fenced enclosure which surrounded it be taken down and re-sited elsewhere. Now I'm no great lover of the cricket establishment, as I am sure you are aware by now, but I could see Ray's threat would cause an almighty rumpus. Move the president's tent? He had to be joking. Oh no, he wasn't. "If you don't get it moved, I'll do it myself", he warned. I suddenly realised he meant business, and I had to stop him. I was forced to give him a lecture. "Be sensible, Ray", I pleaded, "There is no way I am going to get that tent taken down. It stays where it is". "Bugger the president," was his sullen reply.

Eventually he saw sense and wandered back to the Leicestershire dressing-room in a foul mood. Play began on time and, as the president and his honoured guests got stuck into their drinks, I had a little chuckle to myself about how close they had come to having their private party shattered by the visiting captain – all because of a boundary dispute.

Clive Lloyd is one of the gentlemen of the game, but he would be the first to admit it is not a difficult job leading a side as crushingly powerful as his West Indies side of the 1970's and 80's. Every other captain in the world would have loved to swap places and have that battery of fast bowlers to use at their whim. Clive found it a whole new ball game when he led Lancashire briefly. Without the same frightening resources, Clive found captaincy an altogether tougher prospect. I like Clive and I am not in any way degrading him when I say that Brearley was streets ahead. Remember when Brearley was recalled to lead England in 1981 with Australia one up after two Tests? England, thanks to some spectacular individual performances from Botham and Bob Willis, ended up winning the series 3-1 from a seemingly hopeless position. Brearley's part in all this has been obscured by the achievements of Botham and Willis, but I believed his leadership was the key to a fascinating series. Was he lucky? Or was he magnificent? I believe his recall was the turning point. He was a great captain and others in his era were a fair bit behind, even if they had better players to deal with.

Lloyd was involved in one of the ugliest incidents of my umpiring career. I was on the Test panel by then and West Indies were playing England at Old Trafford after the first two matches in the series had been drawn. England had obviously decided that players of proven ability against fast bowlers were the best men to deal with the lethal speed of Mike Holding, Daniel and Andy Roberts. That was why John Edrich, Brian Close and David Steele formed the backbone of the batting even though they were all past their prime.

England had done well to come out of the matches at Trent Bridge and Lord's with honours even, but it was a different story at Old Trafford when time finally caught up with the old stagers. The West Indies had scored a very moderate 211 in the first innings, for which they had Gordon Greenidge to thank for 134 of them. But then Holding, Roberts and Daniel ran riot, ripping out England for 71. It was pitiful to watch from my position as umpire. Not surprisingly, England were a demoralised outfit when the West Indies went in to bat again and, with Greenidge scoring another century, the West Indies set them well over 500 to win by the time

Lloyd declared late on the third evening, leaving England a nasty last half an hour or so to negotiate before stumps were drawn. Only the Lancashire weather or a desperate defensive performance from the England batsmen could prevent the West Indies going ahead in the series.

Close and Edrich had a few uncomfortable overs to face that Saturday evening with the prospect of having to bat for two full days to avoid defeat. England were in trouble, and Lloyd's men knew it. Holding and Daniel were well aware of what they had to do and they began a fearsome barrage of bumpers. The umpires had no directions from the TCCB about the number of bouncers allowed in each over. Any ruling on intimidation was left to us. It was a top class display of fast bowling. Close and Edrich did extraordinarily well to survive, using every ounce of their vast experience to prevent the West Indies making a vital breakthrough before the end of play.

Holding, in particular, was terrifyingly fast, and accurate with it! Brian stood up to all this as only he could. He intercepted these missiles with every part of his body, sometimes choosing to let the ball, propelled at nearly 100 mph, hit him when it would have been easier to use his bat. I well remember the pictures in the newspapers of his torso covered in black bruises a day or two later, and there was no doubting his bravery. It was his idea of blunting the fastest attack in the world, though I am convinced he was a victim of his own publicity. Before the Test series, those same papers he had posed for, had pointed out that the only reason he and Steele were in the England team was to present a morale-destroying straight bat to the West Indian fast bowlers. It may have worked for the first two Tests, but that Saturday evening at Old Trafford Close and Edrich were going through hell. It is said that Close was spitting blood when he returned to the sanctuary of the dressing-room. I had no evidence of this, but he was lucky not to have been seriously injured as the West Indian bowling grew still more ferocious.

I believe the attack on Close may have been deliberate. If so, it certainly succeeded. As the number of bouncers grew and the

71

Standing the Test of Time

batsmen became more disconcerted, I started to worry for the first time that the short stuff was being overdone. I realised I would soon have to intercede. How much longer could I let it continue? Holding provided the answer as he began a new over at my end. Down went three bouncers in succession. The booing around the ground was by now quite intense. I stopped him as he turned to walk back to his mark. "Now look," I said, "this has got to stop, you are taking this too far". Holding shrugged his broad shoulders and looked in the direction of his skipper. Clive Lloyd came over. I told him: "This has got to stop. In my view this is intimidation". Lloyd needed no persuasion. Nor were there any tantrums. He turned to me in his quiet way and told me: "You're the boss. Let's get on with the game". I was very relieved a nasty little incident had been safely resolved.

I suppose what convinced me to act was the sight of poor old Edrich soon after he had been struck in the thigh. With about five minutes of play remaining, he hobbled over in my direction and said, "How do you play these bastards?" As he rubbed the wound his anger and dismay were still very apparent. "I am going to tell the England selectors what they can do with their bloody job", he added. I told him that if he did it would be the last time he played for his country. John had been a loyal and respected servant during 77 Test matches. He was now 39. He never played for England again.

At the end of the game, the England captain Tony Greig called me aside. "Bill," he said, "I have marked you well for your performance during this match, but I want to make an observation". I wondered what he was going to come up with. He went on: "You were wrong to allow Holding to bowl one too many overs of the short-pitched deliveries. You should have stopped him earlier". I was a bit surprised. So I asked him a simple question: "What would you have done as skipper if Holding had been on your side? Would you have taken him off or told him not to cut out the bouncers?". Greig took my point. "I would have done exactly what Clive did," he said. I felt sorry for Greig because he had no real answer to the

West Indies pace men. Lloyd's men were one up with two Tests to play and it was fairly obvious that England were a shell-shocked outfit when they left Old Trafford at the end of the game. Lloyd was beginning to make them grovel!

In my many years on the umpires' list, this was one of the more difficult incidents with which I was required to deal. It is not easy to decide the difference between a legitimate delivery within a legitimate tactic and blatant intimidation. I am satisfied the West Indies had made up their minds to let Close and Edrich "have it" that evening, but there was nothing in the rules to say they could not have bowled six bouncers an over if they so chose. In the end, I am glad common sense prevailed and I am glad also that both Holding and Lloyd knew and accepted that I had to draw a line.

7
Test Debut

I HAVE NO HESITATION in declaring that the large amounts of money involved with cricket these days has made the job of an umpire so difficult as to be almost impossible at times. The pressures are enormous. I never thought I would say this but after 16 years of dealing with the world's best players, I wasn't sorry to reach the end. All right, I was getting on and my knees had been giving me hell over the last few seasons, but apart from having to say goodbye to many friends, I heaved a sigh of relief when I finally quit the game which had been my life for 40 years or more.

I do not intend to bite the hand which has fed me since Somerset made it clear they saw no future for me, but it has to be said that the job of a first-class umpire the day I retired in 1984 was totally removed from the pleasant task it had been when I started. And for this state of affairs I can only pin the blame on the pressures created by the need of every county and international side to get a slice of the cash. Much as I loved cricket, if I had known what the game would be like when I retired, I might well have thought twice about going on to the list at the fairly advanced age of 50. Indeed, I was highly flattered to be so readily accepted as an umpire having been the scourge of them all my life. I suppose it was the cricketing equivalent of a soul repenting or, more likely, a poacher turned gamekeeper.

It was made clear to me that while I might have thought of myself as ready to embark on my fourth career in cricket, it would be short-lived if I did not quickly come to terms with the demands and disciplines of umpiring. I was told in no uncertain terms that, welcome though I was in the umpires' fold, I had only one short summer to prove I was capable of making the grade. These days, many former players are obliged to wait a year or two before they are accepted as umpires. Others are obliged to serve an apprenticeship in lesser competitions like the Minor Counties. That was why I was both surprised and delighted to be taken on as a first-class umpire immediately without any training or background, other than that I had been a player of course. I was confident I could do the job. I would not have applied if I had not been completely sure I was ready for what is an arduous task, standing up and concentrating on every ball that is bowled, day after day for five long months. It sounds easy - idyllic even - but I can assure you it is not. It was only when Lord's gave me the nod of approval that I suddenly came to realise what I had let myself in for, and the few winter months waiting for my debut made me increasingly nervous, like an actor waiting in the wings for his cue.

It was nice to know that I could still be involved in cricket and that my parting of the ways with Somerset had not driven me out of the game. I suppose I might have ended up coaching at a school or club, but I know I would have missed the day-to-day involvement of the top domestic level and my elevation to the umpires list had opened up a new avenue to Test cricket. No promises were ever made, but I was told that my Australian birth would have no detrimental effect if ever I became successful enough as an umpire to be considered for a position on the Test panel. I must admit that sort of news provided a great incentive as I embarked on my new job in the short, white coat. I was a jovial, talkative, easy-going character as a player and I had no intention of changing my whole attitude to life just because I was now in a position of authority.

Far from it, I was encouraged to be friendly and communicative and, to the end, I was still rabbiting on to any player within earshot, though I was still concentrating as hard as ever. I never found concentration any problem, no matter how important or trivial the match, because I loved the game and wanted to be part of it. As a player I liked nothing better than to be either batting or bowling so that being out in the middle for six hours every day as an umpire held no great terrors as far as I was concerned. In the old days, umpiring was a thankless and poorly paid role for former players and it wasn't a job which was too taxing. Players, even in the Test matches, did not put pressure an umpire by constant appealing and the whole business was conducted in an easy and friendly manner, no matter what the state of play.

Some of the umpires in action when I first came on to the list would not have lasted five minutes today. It has to be said, many of them let their minds wander and, from my position as the other official, I saw some very eccentric decisions. I remember as a player a match at Yeovil in which Dai Davies, a Test umpire, made one of the most extraordinary judgements I had ever come across and yet it was accepted by all the players without the slightest hesitation. Harold Stephenson was batting and he deflected a rising ball on to his forehead and the ball looped gently to mid-off where the catch was held without the least difficulty. Stephenson collapsed in pain and medical help had to be dispatched from the dressing-room. It was some minutes before Stephenson regained his senses and his feet. As he lingered in his crease gathering his wits, a polite inquiry came from mid-off and the bowler. "Excuse me, Mr. Davies. Howzat?". Davies looked aghast that anyone should even contemplate such an ungracious appeal. "Come on lads," he remonstrated, "I can't give him out for that, he's been injured.".

Everyone, except the confused Stephenson, knew he was out, but there was absolutely no question of any kind of dissent when Davies made his sympathetic decision. Imagine a similar incident happening today in a first-class match. Davies was one of the best of his era, but I wonder what he would have made of the way in which the modern game is played. I venture to suggest he would hardly recognise it now. That's what the advent of money has done. He would have been sickened by the ludicrous, non-stop appealing, the sloppiness of the players, their lack of manners, the sullen and slow acceptance by a batsman of an lbw decision which has gone against him.

In soccer it is possible for a referee to take an offender's name. Perhaps the time has come for something similar in cricket because dissent, if not verbal, is now a widespread practice. How many times do you see a batsman struck on the pads look every way except at the umpire and shuffle around his crease as the fielding side erupt in a combined appeal? Is that not dissent? I used to say to these lads: "Look at me, son, and I'll give you out". I remember trying to attract the attention of one such victim. He was out all right, but he did not want to stare me in the eyes for the big decision. He had wandered about five yards out of his crease, inspected his bat, his cap, the lot. Eventually I was forced to raise my voice. I shouted: "Oi, I'm over here, and the pavilion is over there". He got the message.

When I started it was altogether nicer. To a certain extent my reputation as a player stood me in good stead. I like to think I was respected and liked and the transition was rather more comfortable than I had anticipated. I think I worried too much when I first became an official. I found it difficult to get a proper night's sleep – and so did my missus. I carried on umpiring even when my head had hit the pillow. According to Betty, I would count in my sleep 1-2-3-4-5-6 as every imaginary delivery was bowled in my dreams. She was prepared to put up with this as she attempted to get some sleep alongside me in bed. But even she had to draw the line when I started signalling wides and leg-byes. I don't think either of us had a full eight hours until I had begun to calm down and to learn my new craft. Those early days were not easy, but once I began to relax and enjoy the game again from my new vantage point the old enthusiasm returned and I came to love my new role every bit as much as I had when playing. My first year was an anxious one. No one likes being on trial but, safely negotiated, I was on my way again.

If my initiation was relatively peaceful, the mood in top-class cricket soon began to change – for the worse. As the older, more established captains and senior players disappeared from the scene, they were replaced by men who were far more uncompromising in their approach. In England it was not long before the Benson and Hedges limited-over cup competition was added to the Gillette Cup, the John Player Sunday League and the County Championship. Sponsors were falling over themselves to put up the money and the players, even before Packer, began to feel the sort of benefits which would have made their predecessors of even ten years before highly envious.

The new breed of captain was far more professional in the proper sense of the word. They wanted to win and to do so often depended on the umpire's decision. The ability to concentrate every second of a match became vitally important as my reflexes and those of my colleagues were tested like they had never been tested before. I saw umpires, particularly inexperienced ones or those without much of a background in county cricket, tried out and then quietly destroyed. The captains have the ultimate answer with the marking system, which can literally make or break an umpire's career. I soon discovered that if the players didn't like a certain umpire, he was as good as finished. No umpire today will last more than a season if the players, whose mouthpieces are the captains, happen not to like or rate them. It is a sad reflection on the way the game has gone and I am only glad I am not starting out again at this particular juncture of the game's history.

I often felt there should be far greater communication between umpires and captains. One of the worst aspects of the marking system is that an umpire is never told what he has been doing wrong. It could be something like standing in a bad position for a fielder's throw. It could be something far more serious. But the umpire will get his marks never knowing where or why he has transgressed. Little wonder some umpires err on the side of safety when it comes to making important decisions. Little wonder also that the confidence of some is never very high. I am sure many umpires would welcome, not to say relish, a quiet word when their marks are low. How else are they supposed to learn? The game's authorities have done much in recent years to improve liaison between players and officials and I know they will take this criticism in the spirit intended. We all have the interests of the game at heart and now that the pressure on umpires is greater than ever, a greater exchange of views might eliminate some of the problems and causes for concern without denigrating the authority of the match officials.

I discovered that my record, as player and umpire, meant nothing as every new season came and went. It meant nothing that I had played first-class cricket with a fair degree of success in Australia and England, or that I had gone on to stand in ten Test matches. A new generation of young player knew little of any of that and probably did not care. To them I was simply a man in a short white jacket who said yes or no to their appeals. I do not resent that. Nor am I surprised. To the very end it made me realise that my reputation no longer went before me. I had to be on top of my job all of the time, as the players expected me to be.

But returning to my first few summers on the list, I found I had an aptitude for the job and, without ever being remotely ambitious, always felt that there had to be a chance I would be elevated to the Test panel. It was the first time in my cricket career that I actually set myself a target. Until then I had simply taken whatever had come my way in terms of any step up in grade. Nevertheless, while I had a family growing up at home, I was just happy to still be doing the round of county grounds, meeting old friends and making new ones. No one could have been more content with his lot. My marks from the captains on the circuit were reasonable without ever being brilliant and I was never at the centre of any controversy which might have led to bad reports. From what I could make out of my own progress, I was above average but not obviously destined for the top.

So it was a wonderful surprise when in the winter before the start of the 1974 season, with a five-year apprenticeship behind me, that I got a call out of the blue from Lord's. Brian Langley, the TCCB's assistant secretary, was on the other end of the line. "I am pleased to tell you, you're on the Test panel. Congratulations!" I think I all but dropped the receiver in stunned amazement. I had no idea I was even close to selection. I could make neither head nor tail of my sudden rise to fame and yet, there I was, a Test match umpire at the age of 55. All through my cricket career I had been something of a late starter. A state player at 26 when many of my Australian contemporaries were thinking of retiring; a county cricketer for the first time at 38 when many had already retired; an umpire at 50 and now, ten years short of my pension, I had at last reached the top. Who said; "Everything comes to he who waits"? Anyway, I came off that phone in a lather of sweat. Indeed, I all but burst into tears; I was so overcome with emotion. Betty and I collapsed into each other's arms and then I went off to fetch a bottle or two of champagne. Never has the bubbly tasted better. It was the culmination of half a century living and breathing the game. As I downed the champagne, I reflected what a great honour had been accorded me. But the thought kept recurring. What had I done to deserve it?

The six umpires on the Test panel were Dickie Bird, David Constant, Charlie Elliott, Arthur Fagg, Tom Spencer and myself. All of them had handled international matches, even Constant, who at 32 was something of a precocious talent. Spencer was 60 and had had a rather strange career at the top level, despite his eminence as the longest-serving umpire on the list. He had first stood in a Test way back in 1954, but in the next 19 years had only been on duty another seven times. Charlie Elliott at 62, and Arthur Fagg, who was 58, were both highly experienced, while Bird, then 41, had three Tests behind him. Nothing was guaranteed. Just because I was on the panel, it did not necessarily follow that I was bound to stand in one of the matches that summer during which England were taking on India and then Pakistan. I had an anxious wait as the season unfolded, hoping to get the call which would give me the chance to show if I was really good enough to be among the top six umpires in the country.

Eventually, and to my eternal relief, it came. With Elliott, who had 40 Tests already under his belt, I was to stand at Edgbaston in the third match of the series against India. I don't think I have ever looked forward more to a match, though with a curious mixture of anticipation and concern. I suppose nothing will ever surpass actually playing in a Test match, but this was an honour which had to be earned just as much, and no one who ever umpires in a Test match will ever look upon it as merely another game. It was as high as I could go in my profession and I was both proud and elated when I arrived at Edgbaston for the match.

To all intents and purposes, as far as the build-up was concerned, it might just have been an ordinary county fixture. There was no question of anyone in authority issuing the umpires with any special orders, nor were Charlie and I treated any differently. Charlie told me to enjoy myself and relax. He said I should pretend it was just another fixture to be safely negotiated and that I would not have been chosen to officiate if many top people in the game had not wanted me to do so. I took him at his word, but even so I was a nervous man when I walked out for the start of the match. Here I was, a foreigner, in charge of an English Test match. What would they be thinking of me back home in Australia? What worried me more than anything was the presence of the evil eye of television. It is never pleasant to think that every decision is going to be dissected again and again by experts; to have your work exposed as wrong in front of millions. It is still more scary when the match is your first, as it was for me that day at Edgbaston.

Elliott was kind enough to give me choice of ends and I thought it best to get involved immediately by taking the first ball of the match, which was to be bowled by Geoff Arnold of Surrey. I gave Sunil Gavaskar his guard and, with just a hint of nerves, called "play".

Gavaskar has been one of the most talented and consistent run-scorers in the history of the game and, in due course, overhauled Sobers and Boycott to become Test cricket's most prolific batsman. The last thing I expected of him was to get out to the first ball of my debut match. But he did, and I was in no position to take much part in it. Arnold thundered in and cut back his first delivery which Gavaskar tried to avoid but could not. The ball appeared to run along the bat and Alan Knott held the catch about six feet down the leg-side. At the time, I was still nervously fumbling the coins in my pocket which I used to count the number of deliveries bowled in each over. There was an appeal and I was lifting my hand from my pocket to give him out, like a gun from a holster, but Gavaskar had decided to take the law into his own hands. Before I had the chance to make history, he had put his bat under his arm and was on his way to the pavilion. He had given himself out and so deprived me of a little piece of glory.

Apparently, it would have been a record for a debut-making umpire to have sent a batsman packing from the first ball of the Test. Had he stood his ground for a couple of seconds, the record would have been mine indisputably. But since he had departed without me being called to adjudicate, I cannot claim it as my own. Far be it from me to criticise a batsman for walking when he knows he is out, but in this case it left me fuming. It was a flat, easy-paced wicket and the one thing I had banked on was Gavaskar, of all people, getting his head down and taking full advantage of the conditions. He had caught me unawares and I have cursed him every time we have crossed paths. I told him afterwards: "Stay still before I give you out".

Sunny is a pleasant, dedicated character and he has always seen the funny side of the incident. Whenever he was with me he smiled. "I'll walk!" he would say in mock threat. Seriously, it was always a pleasure to deal with someone like Gavaskar because he would go if he thought he was out. The vast majority of batsmen would have stayed rooted to their crease and I could have had the pleasure of raising my finger. Television replays showed that Gavaskar was well and truly out. They also showed Bill Alley well and truly caught napping. It was an incredible way to begin my career as a Test umpire and, since it all passed without controversy, my nerves – such as they were – were settled and the rest of the match passed off without further incident, much as I had hoped it would. David Lloyd of Lancashire relished the wicket and the innocuous Indian bowling, scored 214 and booked himself a place on the ill-fated winter tour of Australia.

Talking of counting deliveries, that part of my job was made easier when I got an unexpected present from a brewery representative I met at a dinner. Most umpires have lucky stones or coins with which to count the number of balls bowled during an over. Elliott, for instance, had a little collection of foreign coins which had been part of his working equipment for most of a long and distinguished career. One day he lost one, and when something of such sentimental value is missing it hurts almost as much as if it was worth a lot of money. Charlie searched his pockets, his bag, my bag, absolutely everywhere. He was perplexed and anxious. He traced his every step in a bid to find this coin. I did my bit to help but it all looked like a lost cause. Charlie was inconsolable. Then, in one last attempt to be reunited with his beloved treasure, he went back out on to the pitch. And there it was. Beautifully cut in two by the groundsman's motor-mower!

I never had such a problem, thanks to my meeting with this Watney's rep. I am president of the Mendip Acorns Cricket Club, a fine bunch of people who raise a bit of money for charity and who thoroughly enjoy themselves in the process. It was at one of their end-of-season dinners that I first came across some miniature red barrels. They were tiny, light to hold and different. I expressed an interest in the barrels and the rep said he would send me some in the post. Sure enough, a little package arrived with 72 of them and I have always been grateful. There were about 66 more of them than I had expected, but, as Charlie discovered, it is easy to lose them.

For the rest of my career I always carried a pocketful of red barrels and they became a sort of trademark for me. Other umpires became fascinated by them. After all, if they were ever dropped on the ground, they were always easy to find. David Evans, who later rose to the Test panel, and Mervyn Kitchen, the former Somerset player, were both so keen on them that I gave them each a handful, thereby establishing a sort of cult of the red barrel on the county circuit. When I retired, the barrels were laid to rest. They, too, had been retired.

Sometimes, of course, an umpire errs by allowing an extra ball to be bowled, or even by calling "over" after only five deliveries. It is easily done. But top-class players have a right to expect the highest standards from the officials, and that means counting from one to six properly. The limited overs matches are the easiest in which to make a counting error with the ball flying in all directions. Concentration is vital at all times, even when an umpire is dodging throws from fielders, or even when, as happened, there are appeals at both ends simultaneously. Even so, I always took care of my red barrels and they came to mean as much to me as my boots.

Anyway, returning to my first Test, the rest of the game passed smoothly with plenty of runs being scored on one of those typically fine Edgbaston wickets. I had acquitted myself well on my debut and my marks gave me cause for satisfaction. When I was first told I was to join the Test panel, I was informed that I was a strong character who was liable to give firm, clear decisions at the big occasion. I bore it in mind that this was what the bosses at Lord's were looking for, and I made sure that any decision I made was done so with the utmost clarity. All through my days as an umpire, I even told a batsman verbally when he was out. I would raise my finger and say: "That's out". That way, the batsman never had any doubts. Some umpires have been accused of giving indistinct signals. In fairness to the players and the spectators a signal should be clear, however long it takes to be given. My only proviso is that the batsman, in turn, takes some notice of the decision, particularly if it is given against him. Some players stare at the ground and refuse to take any notice at all. Others, like a certain Mr.Gavaskar, give themselves out and hurry off to the pavilion. Much as I would have liked him to stay for my verdict, I only wish there had been more like him during my time as an umpire.

8
Controversy

IF MY DEBUT TEST passed off without great incident, the same could not be said for my next one, the Third Test against Pakistan at the Oval later that same summer. I was pleased to be given a second chance, the obvious implication being that I had made a success of the first job at Edgbaston. The last thing I expected from this match was any kind of confrontation, but that was exactly what I got!

On the face of it, England versus Pakistan was not the sort of fixture to strike terror in the heart of an umpire and I can only confirm that I was looking forward eagerly to rounding off my initial season on the Test panel with a comfortable five days at the Surrey headquarters.

In those days Pakistan had plenty of quality batsmen and, with Zaheer Abbas in his prime, they built up a massive total of 600 before declaring with only seven wickets down. Zaheer, the record book shows, won himself many admirers with a seemingly effortless 240, made with the sublime timing which was to prove his hallmark. Such a figure would normally have daunted any side batting second, but the Oval wicket was playing perfectly and the Pakistani bowling, with the young Imran Khan coming on second change, did not match the batting for class. As a result, England took their time about building a substantial reply and, from my point of view, it was very often just a case of counting deliveries and making sure a certain drawn match was carried out to its conclusion with the minimum of fuss and bother. Dennis Amiss scored 183 and then Keith Fletcher began to dig in as the England first innings total made its inexorable way past the follow-on target and beyond.

For the best part of four days absolutely nothing of any consequence happened. If ever a match was doomed to complete stalemate, this was it. It began to look as if neither side would get around to batting a second time. Pakistan had taken their time amassing a huge tally and England were well on the way to doing precisely the same. It would have been easy to let the mind wander had this been an ordinary county match. Only the noise and occasional buzz of interest which inevitably accompanies a Test match separated this from the run-of-the-mill.

Then, without warning, just before tea on that fourth day, the whole affair blew up – and Dickie Bird and I were slap-bang in the middle of it all. One minute I was quietly contemplating what I was about to receive for my tea; the next, Bird and me were at the centre of a diplomatic incident. Even the crowd, dozing in the sun, were stirred into life as players started to square up to one another, and we had to do something about it – fast.

I suppose when a volatile character like the Pakistani pace bowler Sarfraz Nawaz is involved, anything can happen at any time. It was just that in the tepid circumstances, a potential fight was the last thing we had a right to expect. Bird was at the bowler's end as Sarfraz came in for the last over before the break with his usual determination and fierce commitment. Fletcher and Tony Greig were at the crease and the England total was creeping up towards that of Pakistan's.

Now Sarfraz was a big lad who needed plenty of time to build up a rhythm as he came in to bowl. In the end he delivered the ball at above medium pace, but he is not the most athletic of men and his run-up is crucial to the delivery, unlike many of the West Indian fast men who can bowl, it seems, at the same phenomenal speed off any kind of improvised run-up. In the case of Sarfraz, it is different. He likes to get everything right as he comes in to bowl and, with England well entrenched, he needed all the help he could get.

Many of the spectators behind the bowler's arm had obviously decided they had seen enough and started to rise from their seats to join the queues for refreshments. Since there had hardly been an incident worthy of the name for three and a half days, I reckon many of them had reasoned they were not likely to miss much now by leaving their places in the last over. Sarfraz was coming in to bowl when the inevitable disturbance behind the bowler's arm led Fletcher to ask Sarfraz to halt his run. The big Pakistani was not amused by this unscheduled interruption. His displeasure at both the offending spectators and Fletcher was evident as he slowly plodded back to his mark again. Indeed, he threw the ball to the ground, put his hands on his hips and snorted like an aggravated bull. It was obvious he had lined up something special for the batsman they call the "gnome" on the county circuit the next ball and, sure enough, he tore into the wicket, ready to give it all he had got.

The result was a fast full toss which Fletcher was glad to turn away for a single. There were obviously some mutterings going on between Sarfraz and Fletcher as the batsman reached the bowler's end, but from my position at square leg it was difficult to tell quite what was said. That single took the giant figure of Tony Greig down to face the music. Sarfraz was upset and furious. I began to feel uneasy. What was going to happen next? Sarfraz went back to his mark and thundered in again. Little did we realise that his next ball would provoke a row which lingered for days and, in the process, turned a slumbering, inconsequential Test match into one which has not been easily forgotten.

Sarfraz lumbered in and delivered a head-high beamer, which Greig appeared to see only at the last split second and managed to avoid by the skin of his teeth. Greig was both shocked and furious and called out at the bowler. Fletcher chipped in and, before Bird and I knew what had happened, we had a fight on our hands. Bird, who like me had been enjoying the match until then, was forced to step between batsman and bowler before the little argument developed further. "I really thought blows were going to be exchanged," he told me later in the sanctity of the umpire's dressing-room. I don't think either of us have been more glad to see a tea interval, which followed, mercifully, in a matter of minutes with Sarfraz, Fletcher and Greig still tossing insults and threats around as they walked from the field.

Standing the Test of Time

The man most affected by this strange, unseemly incident was poor old Dickie, a conscientious and diligent umpire if ever there was one. Dickie was beside himself with grief, blaming himself for allowing the battle to develop. "Did I do right?" he pleaded, pulling his handkerchief from his pocket as he started to cry. Full of sympathy as usual, I told him he had not. I said the trouble had been simmering for some time during that last over and a quiet word from him might have stopped it getting out of hand. Bird spent the rest of that interval fighting his tears as he came to realise we had trouble on our hands.

Needless to say, the Press were quick to seize the opportunity of turning it all into a sensational story. And that is exactly what it was – a sensational story. Before we had been given time to drink our tea, a little cluster of reporters gathered outside our door with a string of questions about the little "war". Dredging some expletives from my Australian locker, I informed them neither of us was prepared to answer queries, not that Bird was in any state to give an account of himself. I suppose I cannot blame the reporters. The match had dawdled on for days without anything except Zaheer's fabulous innings to get worked up about. Now they had a good tale on their hands and they intended to make the most of it. The whole incident was in danger of escalating beyond its true size. I wondered what we could do next to defuse the situation.

Luckily, Sarfraz saw the error of his ways and, probably under some pressure from the Pakistanis, was man enough to come forward and apologise. "I am sorry," he said, "I let it all get to me and exploded. Please forgive my indiscretion." Bird was particularly pleased to hear this, but the last session was played out in a mood of anti-climax and, at the end of the day, the Press were back in force, demanding to know all about that one crazy over. Once again, I refused to talk and Bird stuck to his vow of silence. But it was up to us, the umpires, to smooth it all out between the major protagonists so I set about the task of organising the peace.

From the umpire's room I telephoned the two dressing-rooms and spoke to both Greig and then Intikhab. I told Greig that Sarfraz had offered his apologies and that I expected the same from him. To his credit, he readily agreed it had all gone too far and promised not to continue his feud. As far as he was concerned, it was all over and they would start again next day, if not the best of friends, then certainly not enemies. Intikhab, as Pakistani captain, could hardly draw a veil over the whole sorry affair quickly enough. That achieved, we returned to complete the formality of a drawn match. Fletcher went on to make 122 which, at the time, was the slowest first class hundred ever made in England, almost nine hours of grim defence. Greig, for the record, was bowled by Intikhab for 32 and England were all out for 545 with Sarfraz not having the best of matches, ending with one wicket for 103 runs. Pakistan batted out time with 94 for four in their second innings.

Both Bird and I were glad to see the back of that match. But I like to think our prompt action in defusing a potentially dangerous incident prevented an official reprimand for those players at the centre of the battle, which in turn would have only fuelled the controversy still further. The players concerned were fortunate not to have been fined, or even banned. Perhaps they should have been. Yet in the context of a dull draw, it was right that the whole thing should have been forgotten – and quickly. From my point of view, it was a testing way to end my first season on the panel, and I hope my part in bringing to an end an affair which reflected badly on some fine cricketers did not go unnoticed by the powers at Lord's. My reappointment for the 1975 season appeared to confirm their approval.

Most disappointingly, both Greig and Fletcher were players I had admired and, in spite of this blemish, continued to rate highly, particularly as captains. In time, Greig and Fletcher were given the chance to lead England and, in their differing styles and methods, they each had a measure of success. Greig, of course, came to be vilified in England for his part in the formation of Packer's alternative cricket, but this tends to detract from his achievements as captain of his adopted country. I would go so far as to say he was one of the best. Greig had the respect and loyalty of those who served him, especially when he was leading England. One of his players told me once: "Tony never expects anything of a player unless he had done it first. He will ask us to field in a close position, for instance, only because he had stood close to the bat himself". In short, he led from the front with a zest and enthusiasm and, indeed, with a competitiveness not always matched by his successors. Tony wanted to win and was prepared to battle hard from the first ball of a Test match until the last. When Tony Greig was in charge, England didn't surrender readily.

Greig was not always well equipped in terms of having outstanding players to work with, but he earned my respect by the aggressive way he approached his job, particularly against Ian Chappell's Australians. Chappell had Lillee and Thomson in their primes, Greig had only John Snow as an answer, but it did not stop him taking the fight to the Aussies. Snow was an exceptional bowler in my estimation and, like Greig, was not always given the applause he merited, I suppose because he was no stranger to controversy, nor was he a favourite of the game's establishment. If Greig had another bowler of Snow's quality, England would have been a strong team under his leadership. Greig, like Brearley, did not allow the game to drift. He was always experimenting, maybe only for an over or two, and always working on ways of making a breakthrough. To the spectator, Greig's constant field-changing and gesticulating might have been a source of irritation because he was always holding up play to get everything right. But to those of us involved out on the field, he was an inspirational captain who made his changes for a purpose. He was always trying something new, and with top-class players he might have gone down in history as an exceptional international captain. Unfortunately, he will now only ever be remembered for World Series Cricket. As a man, a player and as a leader, I remember him with affection. He was my type of cricketer.

Talking of Snow, I am reminded of an incident at Eastbourne in Sussex. Off the field Snowy is an amiable sort of character but he took his cricket seriously on the field and there was no more determined competitor. Sometimes, of course, it got him into trouble.

He could give the impression of being surly and uncommunicative, which did not help his cause, but I never found him less than 100 per cent committed. He took as much care over his batting as he did with his bowling, though it was as a fast bowler that he made his name. Snow was batting in a county match when I gave him out from my position at square leg as he lunged forward in a desperate attempt to make his ground when going for a quick run. I was positive he was a goner. Up went my finger. "That's out Snowy," I told him. John did not approve of my decision and his displeasure was evident for all to see. He put his hands on his hips and then made a slow journey back to the pavilion, muttering to himself en route. With decisions like that, there is always scope for controversy. It all happens in a split second. But I was in the best position and it was me who had to decide whether he was out or not. I had no doubts. That evening John made a point of ignoring me in the bar. He obviously still felt aggrieved about his run out. I told him there was no point in him behaving like that, I was not now going to reverse the decision.

Next day, Snowy was forced to concede. Indisputable evidence came my way which showed, once and for all, that I was right and John was wrong. A spectator had taken a photograph of the incident and he presented it to me for inspection before play. Sure enough, Snow was well out. With a growing feeling of righteousness, I took the picture to the Sussex dressing-room and sought out the culprit. "Take a look at this," I said to him. Snow surveyed the evidence in silence. "You were right," he conceded at last, "but bloody lucky!" John and I have often laughed about that little clash since, but it shows what a competitive sort of character he could be.

It also reveals how cricketers never think they are out! I used to curse umpires when I was a player over lbw decisions and run-outs. Like them, I always thought the official had made a mistake. No batsman is prepared to believe he is out when he lunges forward towards his crease when a run-out is being attempted. And when it comes to leg-before verdicts, the batsman will always say he was too far forward, or that he was outside the line of the stumps, or that he had got a touch to the ball with the bat. All I can answer, in defence of umpires, is that every decision has to be made in a split-second. Contrary to the belief of some cricketers, every decision is made without prejudice. Sometimes an umpire will be wrong, I admit. But luck has a habit of evening itself out and for every decision given against a player, many others given in his favour are just as inaccurate. Players, even at the highest level, should be more philosophical about this. I cannot honestly believe that brooding over a dismissal is going to improve a batsman's health and no kind of dissent will persuade an umpire to reverse his adjudication. I know of no umpire in my experience who has given a batsman out simply because he did not like him, or was in any way prejudiced against him. My advice to cricketers is to accept the rough with the smooth because, spread over a whole series or season, a batsman gets what he deserves. The best players always end at the top of the averages because their greater ability will ultimately shine through.

In 40 years of cricket, I have never come across an unlucky cricketer or, indeed, a lucky one in the sense that the gods seemed to be permanently conspiring against them, or for them. Anyway, I always found Snow to be a tough performer who gave everything for England, in spite of his clashes with authority. In the same way, Geoff Arnold of Surrey was the sort of man who could just as easily upset people by his whole-hearted approach and his fierce determination. I liked both men. Unlike some umpires, I knew that they were playing to win and bore me no lasting grudge if ever an appeal of theirs was rejected. I only wish I had a camera at my disposal more often when Snow was playing!

Snow and Arnold were always difficult bowlers to control, though I should add not for any disciplinary reason. Like Bob Willis, they were prone to no-ball because they made no allowances with their front feet in their delivery stride. In an effort to get maximum pace and to get as close to the batsman as possible, all three were inclined to overstep the mark more often than they will care to remember. I lost count of the number of times I would have to say to them quietly: "You're too close to that line". They would accept this, not as advice to give them an unfair advantage, but as a warning of sorts. They were all good, international-class bowlers who knew what they were doing. They were all prepared to take a chance on being no-balled because they were not the type of player to compromise. But from my point of view as an umpire, they were bad bowlers to officiate. Willis, in particular, was prone to rashes of no-balls if, as he did periodically, he had trouble with his run-up. In fairness to him, he never once disputed my decisions, even if some of his overs were littered with as many as four no-balls.

Willis's record as a bowler, with more than 300 Test wickets in a distinguished career, speaks for itself. As a captain he came in for a lot of criticism and I am forced to admit I often had cause to doubt the quality of his leadership. Whenever I walked out on to the field in a match in which his team, Warwickshire, were involved, it was always hard to tell who was in charge. Everyone except Bob seemed to be talking, gesticulating and organising the field. Bob was an amiable fellow, but he did not impose any sense of authority on the field. Bob was first and foremost a fast bowler who needed all his time and energy to get his own performance right. As an umpire I could sense that he was allowing matters to drift. Sometimes, in the heat of the moment, I would wonder to myself who the hell was in control. I would turn around and spot the Warwickshire skipper with his arms folded at mid-off in a world of his own. I would say; "Come on then Bob, sort this out". He would spring to life and organise his field, but he needed to be reminded at times. I believe he was a captain who led by example, but even his best friends would never hold him up as an outstanding leader.

In England's case there was really no other legitimate candidate for the captaincy and, with limited talent to use, he did not do a bad job. I believe he would have been more successful with both county and country if he had had greater resources. It has to be said also that, although he had a style all of his own, those who played under him rated him highly as a captain. They liked and respected him and, although he never cracked the whip on the field, there were prominent players who thought the world of him.

Standing the Test of Time

Keith Fletcher of Essex was the best captain in the game by the time I came to the end of my career. In my opinion, England made a big mistake getting rid of him so soon. He came back from a tour of India and Sri Lanka in 1982 and was promptly discarded. I could never understand why. For my money he was far and away the best leader in county cricket and should have been leading England for at least another year or two. I am aware of the arguments that at the time of his replacement he was 38 and probably past his prime, but I still think his dismissal was premature.

Unlike Australia, England have always preferred to choose a captain and ten other players. In Australia they pick a team first and a captain later. I am not saying Fletcher was at that stage of his career a Test batsman any longer, but he would have been worth his place for his captaincy alone. I used to marvel at his work with Essex. After many years without achieving anything of note, they suddenly became a power in the county game and I believe Fletcher deserves much of the credit. I will acknowledge that in Graham Gooch, Ken McEwan and John Lever he had some outstanding players at domestic level, but many of the others, with the best will in the world, were ordinary county professionals. Yet Fletcher got the best out of them and still made sure that the team's reputation for enjoying their cricket lived on.

Fletcher took the game seriously enough as a master tactician, switching his field and his bowlers to influence the manner in which a match was going. I cannot think of another captain in county cricket to match Fletcher, although I am sure he would be honest enough to concede that there were several more talented teams, on paper at least. Middlesex, for example, should have won everything. And that is not necessarily a criticism of Mike Gatting, their captain. They had plenty of fast bowlers, like Daniel and Norman Cowans, the two best spinners in England with Edmonds and Emburey and some quality batsmen.

Where other captains would allow a match to drift, Fletcher was always seeking to change proceedings. Perhaps if he had had a greater array of talent he may have sat back and let them get on

94

with it but, because he did not, he was obliged to squeeze what he could from the players at his disposal. The bald truth is that Fletcher handled limited players fantastically and they responded, while I was on the umpire's list, by helping him win an array of trophies under his guidance. It often struck me as strange that while England struggled as a team, and while poor old Willis came in for some fearful criticism for his laid-back style of leadership, that on obscure county grounds in front of the proverbial three men and a dog, Fletcher was quietly weaving his magic, forgotten and rejected.

In spite of Fletcher's competitive nature, Essex maintained a deserved name as a team for whom cricket could be fun. It in no way detracts from their professionalism when I say that they were the jokers in the county game and all the umpires looked forward to handling their games. Of course they wanted to win, and they played as hard as any of their rivals, but they knew how to enjoy themselves on and off the field. Fletcher sensibly allowed them to laugh and joke on the field, but he always knew where and when to draw the line. Lever, Brian Hardie and David Acfield were the prime movers in any form of diversionary amusement, but the chief laughter-maker was the left arm spin bowler Ray East. East was legendary around the county circuit for his pranks and his antics and wrote a highly amusing book about the lighter side of cricket. In my view he was a better player than he allowed himself to be given credit for. Had he taken the game a little more seriously he might have got a little closer to international recognition, but that was not his style. Fletcher never tried to discipline him to my knowledge. He let him have his head and yet was shrewd enough to tap his talent to the benefit of the team.

Even Ray East knew when to stop! East may have been a capable bowler, but he will not mind me saying he was not the bravest batsman in the world - as I discovered at Portsmouth one day in 1977. Hampshire introduced a raw and extremely fast young bowler from the West Indies to the county game. Andy Roberts was a man in a hurry. At the time, fresh from Antigua, he was as fast as any bowler in the world and he was desperately keen to make his place in Clive Lloyd's West Indian team a permanent one. Hampshire could hardly believe their luck as he tore in on their behalf with great hostility and success. East would not have been the only county professional surprised and disconcerted by this weapon Hampshire unleashed on their unsuspecting rivals. This particular day, East was shifting uneasily in his crease as a series of missiles from Roberts threatened to put him in a hospital bed. One such ball struck him on the wrist and flew to the slips where he was safely caught.

At the time, I was convinced the ball had struck him on the arm and, although Hampshire appealed for the catch, I turned them down. I admit I was wrong but, as I have said, all decisions are made on the spur of the moment and in this case I felt he had been struck further up his arm. East was too distressed to care. He was rubbing his wrist furiously and muttering to himself. By the time he was ready to pick up his bat again, he was furious and bewildered to discover he was still in. "I'm out," he pleaded as the prospect of more punishment loomed. "You're not," I told him. "But it hit me on the wrist. The only reason I stayed my ground was because I thought the ball had not carried.".

I told him the ball had carried to the fielder but in my opinion it had struck him on the arm. Anyone else would have been grateful for the extra "life", but not East. The thought of facing Roberts again plainly filled him with terror. His conscience was also troubling him. He did not like the thought that he had conned the umpire by standing his ground. So the next ball he faced, from another bowler, East gave his wicket away, gently touching a catch to the nearest fielder. He could not leave the square quickly enough. Afterwards I tackled him on the curious manner of his exit. "I had to get out," he said with a seriousness all the more surprising coming from such a renowned joker. "I don't like cheating anyone". That was typical of Ray East. I am sure the fearsome Roberts provided an additional incentive to head for the pavilion, but he really was anxious to set the record straight by going immediately. The last thing he wanted to do was acquire any reputation for underhand tactics.

96

Essex were a happy outfit and I enjoyed my matches with them, and it was like them to provide a surprise or two for me right up to the day I retired. At the end of my last session officiating at one of their matches, Fletcher summoned me to their dressing-room. "The lads have got a little present for you," he told me. I could not get in there quickly enough. As the Essex players gathered around, Fletcher gave a little speech thanking me for the good years, the fun and my company. With that he produced a miniature bottle of tonic water and, handing it to me, they all applauded.

I would have liked to say how pleased I was with my present but the size of my farewell gift left me speechless. I did my best to thank them but I should imagine my words did not ring true as I surveyed this bottle of tonic water. I said how much I appreciated...the thought! As I was leaving the room, Fletcher called me back and from under a towel, he produced a bottle containing a gallon of gin. "Put some of this in the tonic," he said. I should have expected something like that from Essex. Only they could have dreamt up such a stunt. They succeeded in embarrassing me, but I did not mind. They played cricket in a good spirit and I was pleased they were also successful. I am not saying the game should be reduced to one long laugh, but if a few other teams took their approach the umpire's life would be easier and more fun. Jokers they may have been, they also knew how to win. Keith Fletcher saw to that.

9
Chappell's Aussies

MY FINGERS WERE CROSSED that I would be retained on the Test panel for 1975. Not only was it the first year of the World Cup, but Australia were scheduled to provide the opposition in four Tests. From the moment I first became an umpire, it had been my ambition to officiate in a Test involving my home country. You will never understand how elated I was when my place among the umpiring elite was confirmed. Even so, with only four Tests that summer, there was no guarantee I would be summoned to stand in one of them. The first match in the series, at Edgbaston, came and went. Every time the telephone rang at home I hoped it would be to tell me I had been selected to stand in a Test. Suddenly it came. "You're on Bill," they said. "England versus Australia at Lord's. Good luck!".

What a moment that was. When it all sank in I felt a strange mixture of great happiness and terror. Indeed, I was still gathering my wits when the phone started ringing again. Inevitably it was the Press. The pressure was just beginning. Normally I am not the sort of bloke who worries too much about anything, but as the big day and the big match approached I could feel myself becoming increasingly tense and anxious. My mind would wander during county matches as I contemplated the enormity of the challenge facing me, and of the unusual pressures. Here I was, an Australian living in England about to act as an adjudicator in a Test match between two countries whose rivalry provided the backbone of the game.

Whose side would I be on? Was I an Aussie or an Englishman now? These were the sort of questions being fired at me from Swansea to Sydney, from Bristol to Brisbane. It seemed the entire world wanted to know how I was going to react. Never before had an Australian umpired a match involving his home country abroad. Never before, I would venture to suggest, had an umpire been put under so much scrutiny. I began to think my part in this forthcoming match was going to be more important than the players. I only wish I could have given everyone a straight answer. But truth to tell, I honestly had no idea how I was going to react. The doubts crept into my mind, especially in the silence of the night. I knew that every decision I made, no matter which side it benefited, would be minutely analysed across the world. Heaven forbid that I was wrong. If I gave a verdict England's way, the Aussies would moan that I was over-compensating. If I gave it in favour of Australia, the inevitable cry of bias would haunt me. I could not win, as I saw it, and I began to realise I would have to go the entire five days without making the wrong choice. I started to feel as if I was being pushed into a corner, and in bad moments as the intensity of the pressure grew, I wished I could have no part of it.

My wife Betty, who knows me better than anyone, realised the occasion was beginning to get to me, but it did not stop me giving her an unjustifiably hard time. The more I thought about it, the worse it became, and I am afraid to say I took it out on poor Betty, snapping her head off at the slightest provocation. There was nothing she could do to help me get through the impending ordeal, but I grew more morose and bad-tempered by the day as the Lord's Test approached. In a strange way the build-up tarnished what, for me, was the high point of my career. As the tension mounted I found sleep virtually impossible and I can only imagine I must have been pretty poor company as the cares of the world heaped upon my shoulders. I think what worried me more than anything was the thought that the match would be seen on television in Australia. I wondered how the Australians were going to take to me, particularly as I had left the country under a sort of cricketing cloud.

I suppose most pressures are self-inflicted, but in this case my fears were deepened by the constant interest being expressed, sometimes said in a jovial, good-natured fashion, about where my loyalties lay. Even so, I kept my thoughts to myself. For a man noted for speaking his mind I surprised myself with my reticence. Uncharacteristically perhaps, I sat firmly on the fence on all questions and waited for the moment to arrive with rapidly diminishing patience. I must also admit to being a little scared of the prospect of handling some of the guys destined to play in the match. Ian Chappell's reputation for his, how shall I put it, aggressive leadership was matched only by Tony Greig's fierce determination to regain the Ashes and to put the nightmare of the 4-1 drubbing in Australia the previous winter firmly behind him. Lillee and Thomson were at the height of their powers, with Thomson's oft-quoted relish for a batsman's blood still very fresh in the minds of us all. I expected the worst. So here I was, coming up to the biggest day of my life, dreading it more than looking forward to it.

Eventually, after what had seemed like a prison sentence in terms of time, the moment arrived. Truth to tell, I was so nervous that I can remember precious little about the journey to Lord's. All I can recall is a curious cacophony of sound as I reached the famous ground and the numerous, well-intentioned good luck wishes. But my trepidation only increased with such comments as: "Don't give too many decisions against us Bill", coming as they did from both English and Australian spectators and supporters. Through their smiles and their ribald laughter I got the impression it was all a bit double-edged. England versus Australia at Lord's is the show-piece of any season. After Australia's crushing win at Edgbaston in the First Test, the match now assumed even greater importance – and I was at the centre of it all.

Lord's was an absolute cauldron that day. Everyone who is anyone seemed to be at the ground. People I had not seen for years leapt out of the shadows with the same veiled greeting. I trotted out the same reply to them all. "I can only do my best. There will be no favouritism." I can remember the heat of the day. Even before I left the sanctity of the umpires' room my shirt was sticking to me. It was the biggest occasion of my life. A packed crowd waited intently. The players were ready. Then the second bell was sounded, summoning the umpires out to begin the action. I could feel my hands trembling slightly and my legs carried me to the door on automatic pilot. I was in a daze of mixed emotions. I now know what it must have been like to walk to the gallows, because if ever a bloke was set up for an execution, it was me. "Good luck Bill," people shouted as I made my way through the Lord's Long Room, surely the most famous inner sanctum in cricket. I could feel the eyes of those famous names forever captured in paintings and pictures on the Long Room walls bearing down and burning through me as I made my way out towards the sunlight. I was proud, exhilarated, nervous and plain bloody scared all at the same time.

The atmosphere was absolutely unbelievable. No one who had never been privileged enough to experience such a moment will ever quite be able to understand the nerve-tingling intensity of it all. I honestly don't remember making my way down those steps from the pavilion out on to the playing area. I was just trying to take it all in without letting myself be intimidated by the sheer mysticism and magnitude it all represented. At the bottom of the steps the noise reached a crescendo as the spectators at the far sides of the ground could see play was imminent, but I was lost in a world of my own.

On the long march to the wicket, it was impossible not to think back to Brooklyn, Sydney, the Lancashire leagues and to Somerset; to the many friends I had made on the path to this sensational day. I thought of Betty and the family. What would they be making of all this? At the crease, the Lord's groundsman Jim Fairbrother was guarding his pride and joy like a dog guarding a bone. It was always his custom, to his dying day, to wait at his wicket until the last possible moment in case the umpires or the players wanted anything else. Jim was a good pal of mine and he knew what this meant to me. He looked at me and smiled. "Good luck mate", he said. The roar of the crowd around us signalled the impending arrival of the Australians, who were fielding first. I felt for my red barrels for comfort as my pulse raced again. Play was about to begin.

Standing the Test of Time

What happened next provided the most unpleasant two hours of my entire career as an umpire. Never in my life had I been subjected to such a barrage of hostile appealing; never in my life had I felt like simply walking off the field in utter disgust. No one need tell me the Australians have always been a team which appeals for everything. I did it myself when I played first-class cricket in my home country. But I simply did not expect anything like the reception Chappell's men gave me in that first session. To appeal is a legitimate part of the game, but Chappell and his boys carried it to ridiculous extremes – and I hold the skipper personally responsible for the whole unsavoury experience.

From the first ball of the morning until the last, the Aussies let me have it with both barrels. They shouted for everything just to see whose side I was on; just to test where my loyalties lay. I am convinced Chappell set me up and I don't think I can ever forgive him. I realise I had no right to expect an easy time. This was an important Test match and I fully anticipated that no quarter would be asked or given. England and Australia have traditionally given nothing away to each other on the cricket field and this was obviously not going to be an exception for my benefit. What I had not anticipated was the sheer ferocity and intensity of the Aussie appealing. It sickened me that they could act in such a way. Every time the ball touched the pads, even via the bat, or every time a batsman played and missed, the entire team leapt and screamed as one. To say the least I was shaken. Nearly every appeal was ludicrous and completely pointless. I suddenly realised they were testing me out and I became very frightened. I believe it would have all been different if Benaud, say, was skipper. He would never have stood for such behaviour. But he was not. Chappell was in charge, and he was roasting me.

Time after time I rejected their claims for a dismissal. I would have needed my head seeing to if I had agreed to some of the things they were asking for, but I knew they were doing it deliberately. It was a hot day and I could feel the perspiration running down my body as the Aussie grilling became more demonic and malicious.

My heart pounded every ball. What would they do next, I kept asking myself. I can tell you it was a relief to take a breather at square leg and I began to dread having to resume my position at the stumps at the end of the overs. Most of the appeals were so outlandish that it was easy to say "no", but I was being put into a carefully-laid trap. By the sheer weight of the appeals I had to give one sooner or later in their favour – and it could well have been the wrong one. Not to have done so would have risked the charge of bias towards England. To have given a bad decision, out of sheer pressure, for the Australians would have brought the wrath of an entire nation on my head with people around England nodding the sentiment: "I told you so, Bill's still an Aussie".

Dennis Lillee was a particularly nasty appealer. He would turn and snarl, lift his finger in mock imitation of an umpire's signal for a dismissal and jump up and down for good measure. He defied you to turn him down, and it needed a man with strong nerves to look him in the eye and reject him. Lillee gave me the full treatment that morning, but I kept saying to myself: "You must not crack. You must not give in to them." Lillee hated batsmen, no matter who they were. But these were the dreaded Poms he was bowling to and, with Ian Chappell winding him up, he was ready to kill for his cause. If ever I no-balled him he would look at me as if I was mad. He would always want to know why or where he had gone wrong, but it was asked in such a way that I knew he was questioning my decision without being blatant about it. Jeff Thomson was coming in from the other end with tremendous speed with that distinctive sling-like action. If ever a batsman was unfortunate enough to play and miss at Thommo he would let forth a torrent of four-letter abuse, some of which not even I had heard before. I honestly don't believe he meant much of it, but, like Lillee, he was so psyched-up that he was behaving abnormally.

For that I suppose Ian Chappell should take the credit. His players thought the world of him as a skipper and they all followed him into battle without a whisper of dissent. Ian was a hard and capable leader and he knew how to get the best out of his men. On this occasion he had obviously decided to play on me as a possible weakness, and I can only say that if his intention was to give me hell, then he certainly succeeded. Now I am no prude and I can dish out the swear words with the most eloquent exponent of the that particular "art", but I must admit I was ashamed at the way the Aussie players swore and gesticulated whenever I rejected an appeal. Perhaps they really believed I had made a whole series of mistakes. More likely it was all part of the ploy to intimidate me into agreeing, eventually, to one of their demands. I am pleased to say that in spite of the provocation, I held firm, though I will never know how. I must say that Greig was no shrinking violet when it came to bad language. He and Ian Chappell raised it to a new level in that match and some of the other England players were not innocent either. England had a bad first session, losing their first four wickets for 49. No wonder the Aussies appealed for everything. When at last stumps were drawn for lunch, I have never felt so relieved. As I made my way back to the pavilion at the end of my ordeal, I felt an arm wrap around my shoulder. It was Ian Chappell.

Chappell was the last person I wanted to see at that particular moment. I knew he had deliberately made my morning a misery, but even I was shocked when he confirmed it all. "Bill, you've come through it well," he told me, "we'll go easier on you from now on". I could hardly believe my ears. Here was the captain of the Australian Test side openly admitting the previous two and a quarter hours of harassment had been a ploy, discussed in the secrecy of their dressing-room and carried out with professional precision on the pitch. I can't remember making a reply, I was so taken aback by what he evidently thought was a conciliatory statement. I brooded for the entire duration of the lunch break.

To say I was disappointed would be an understatement, but I let the matter drop. I reasoned that if I wanted to umpire at this level, and remember this was only my third Test, then I must be prepared to put up with anything. It was all a million miles from the gentle atmosphere of county cricket and I was forced to accept it as part of everyday life at the top. I have never been under greater

*When I first came in as a youngster playing for
Northern Districts (New South Wales)*

Hitting out in the nets at Petersham, Sydney

AUSTRALIAN TEST "PROSPECT"
September 13th 1946

'A "probable" for the forthcoming series of Tests between Australia and the M.C.C. is W. E. Alley of New South Wales This left-hand batsman finished 4th in the batting averages for the inter-state cricket series in 1945-46, with an average of 69.3. Although not a stylish batsman, he posesses a powerful drive and a strong defence. His favourite shot is to square leg.'

P.A. Reuter

An early photograph when I arrived in England

*Receiving wedding presents from Colne Cricket
Club in 1949, after my marriage to Betty*

Reading a scrap album with the family

Signing my contract for Blackpool Cricket Club,
with the Chairman Frank Place looking on

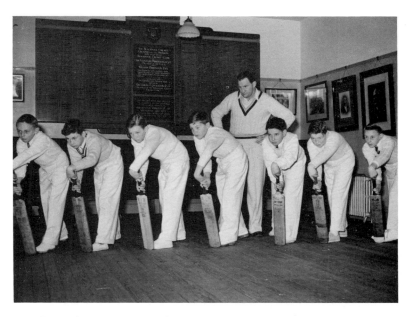

Coaching young boys at Blackpool C.C. 1954

*8th May, 1962. Middlesex v. Somerset at Lord's.
I pull a ball from Don Bennett to the boundary.*

Receiving the Brylcream Trophy as Cricketer of the Year, 1961

Fishing cricket balls from the river at practice at Somerset

A typical Alley sweep to leg

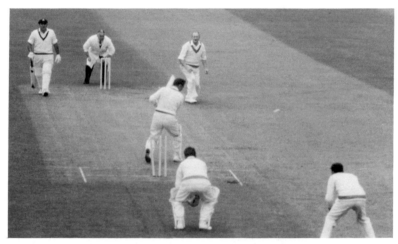

My dismissal of Bobby Simpson, bowled through the gate for five, at Taunton during the Australian tour of 1964. (The umpire was the great Sid Buller)

A perfect cover drive

*Leading out the team at Somerset, August 1964
when captain*

*In action against Sussex in my final season of
1968 (the wicket-keeper is Jim Parks)*

Alley the umpire – Norman McVicker has Peter Willey caught behind

Charlie Elliot and I running for cover at Edgbaston in my first Test Match

Umpiring one of my greatest adversaries, John Snow of Sussex and England

*With Ken Palmer walking out at Taunton in my
last season as an umpire.*

Alley the farmer

pressure, either before or since, but the Chappell incident taught me a valuable lesson. From then on I was no longer to be shocked by anything that happened on the field of play. I was hardened by the experience and a better umpire for having been the victim of a cruel piece of gamesmanship. Now, although I had every right to feel sorry for myself in the circumstances, Ian Chappell and his boys had broken no rules. Even if I had wanted to, there was nothing for which I could have touched him. As far as the book was concerned, Chappell had done everything he should – and that was the end of the matter.

Actually, there was plenty to admire about the man. He was a gritty batsman, lacking the classic style and flair of his brother as a batsman, but was one hell of a captain. I have to say he and Greig were never the best of friends on the field or off it. They squared up to one another in the manner of Connors and McEnroe, never speaking to each other unless they had to and never even looking in the same direction. Both men gave everything for their countries and the clashes of 1975, fuelled by the World Cup earlier in the summer, are unlikely to be equalled for sheer competitiveness.

The afternoon and evening sessions were altogether easier and I slowly stopped feeling sorry for myself and angry with Chappell. Later in the match, with Greig scoring a brave 96 when it mattered most, England began a recovery and, although Lillee finished with a creditable four for 84, England were eventually all out for 315, a figure made all the more satisfactory bearing in mind their appalling start on that ferocious first morning. I slept well that night, my first real sleep for ages. It had been the best – and worst – day of my career.

Snow took four wickets for 66 as the Aussies struggled in reply. At one stage Australia were 81 for seven and the chances of a follow-on were very real indeed. Then Ross Edwards took over, scoring a defiant and responsible 99 and, with Lillee making what proved to be a Test career-best 73 not out, Australia were all out 47 behind. When England batted a second time, John Edrich took advantage of an increasingly benign wicket to master the pace attack of Lillee, Thomson and Walker to make 175, which, after the flak he took in

Standing the Test of Time

Australia in 1974-5, must have been all the sweeter, coming as it did at the hands of the same three bowlers. England were able to declare at 436 for seven, leaving Australia a massive 484 to win. But with Rick McCosker, both Chappells and Edwards again, all getting runs, the Aussies were able to not only avoid defeat but end at 329 for three.

So ended an incredible match from my point of view. It was the realisation of an ambition, but it was achieved at a cost. I was never able to say anything about Chappell that first morning and I don't intend to carry on bleating about it now. What annoys me more than almost anything is that the Australian players did not really need to attempt to intimidate me into jumping into decisions. For a few years either side of 1975 they were probably the best balanced side in the world. They had everything – great fast bowlers, a competent opening pair in McCosker and Alan Turner and plenty of quality batting in the middle order. In Edwards they had an outstanding cover fielder and, under Ian Chappell, a team spirit second to none. Later that year they went home to Australia and crushed Clive Lloyd's West Indians by five Tests to one. At the time they were the holders of the Ashes, drawing twice more after Lord's to win the series 1-0. There was no question that they were the best outfit in international cricket. The West Indies may have won the World Cup that year, but they were still an inexperienced team prone to rashness and it was some time before they emerged as an outstanding squad. Quite why Ian Chappell thought I could help him, I shall never know.

Anyway, it was a relief to get it all over and return to my lair in Somerset to think over the lessons of Lord's. I started to behave like a human being again, now that the pressure was off. I even began to treat Betty with the respect she deserved. I was to officiate at three more England versus Australia, at Old Trafford and Leeds two years later and at Trent Bridge in 1981. The match at Leeds was, of course, laced with as much controversy but it did not affect me in the same way. Shall we say that after Lord's 1975, I was ready for whatever came my way.

106

Greg Chappell was still only a teenager when he came over to England on a two-year contract to play for Somerset. I liked the lad and so did everyone else at the club. His first season at Taunton was my last on the staff and I took him under my wing a little in that summer, which was his first away from home. But our friendship ground to a halt during that same match at Lord's in 1975. I gave him out, leg before to Snow in the Australian first innings. He had only scored four and he was obviously unhappy with my verdict. For the rest of the match, although there was plenty of opportunity, he did not speak to me. Coming from such a gracious and well-mannered man, such an act was all the more difficult to comprehend. Every batsman – and I was no different – is upset by a leg before decision which goes against him, but most of them have to get over their pique. It took a fair time for Greg Chappell to forgive and forget what he must have felt was my blunder. I know I have not been right in every decision I have given. For all I know, I may even have been wrong when I gave Greg out. But the decision was given on the spur of the moment without a television monitor to consult for five minutes to think it over. In this particular case, I feel sure I was right but at least I am honest enough to agree that all umpires err. So do players. I look forward to the day when some of them admit umpires might even be correct on occasions.

That aside, I always got along famously with Greg from the day he arrived in the heart of the west of England to begin his contract. Even from the start he had all the shots, which he carried out in the most extravagant manner. But that same extravagance was often his undoing. Gradually we tightened his technique and by the time he left, two years later, he was a vastly improved performer. He could play on any surface and against any type of bowling and the time he spent at Somerset had much to do with his development into a world class player.

When he came to us, Greg bowled a bit of rather frail leg spin. Far be it from me to discourage anyone to bowl from the back of the hand, but the leg spinner was already on the way out in English cricket. Now he is all but extinct. With the advent of one-day competitions, most counties wanted someone who could bowl tight medium pace to back up the new-ball bowlers and Greg was persuaded to drop his leg spin and take up medium pace. It worked a treat. He became a thoroughly reliable back-up bowler and in his last year at Somerset took 45 wickets with his new style, in first-class cricket alone. I had every sympathy with Greg because I too had been asked to take up seam bowling at the expense of leg spin, which I had enjoyed. When he returned to Australia, the home crowds must have been surprised at the metamorphosis of their great young talent. He returned a different and, I think, better player than when he came over. I know he liked it at Somerset and they were sorry to see him depart.

In many ways Greg was lucky to have his brother still in the national team when he took over the mantle of captaincy. It is never easy to follow a successful leader. When it is your brother you are replacing the job becomes doubly difficult. I am sure Ian was able to offer advice without impairing Greg's freedom to make his own decisions. Greg had a mind of his own but in their style of leadership I found the Chappell brothers remarkably similar. They were both fortunate to have some outstanding players working for them, but they knew how to use them and duly reaped the benefit.

When Chappell stepped down, first as captain and then out of the game, Australia were beginning to slide. The Aussies lost Greg Chappell, Lillee and Rod Marsh all at the same time and there were no obvious top-class replacements. The Australians discovered what had happened in England maybe ten years earlier: that there were fewer and fewer outstanding players in any team outside the West Indies. Some of the cricketers calling themselves internationals or Test players would have had a job getting into a county team when I first started. Standards around the world had dropped alarmingly and, for the first time since the war, Australia didn't have a great player at their disposal. As an Australian it gives me no pleasure to say that, but I am sure any honest observer would have been forced to draw the same, sad conclusion.

In England there was an even bigger shortage of star names. Towards the end of my time on the umpires' list, I was disappointed to see the quality of some of these lads masquerading as county cricketers actually making a living out of the game. I hoped for the sake of both countries that genuine talent, the sort of players who excite the crowds the world over, could be unearthed quickly. Perhaps youngsters today have more distractions; perhaps there is more to do. When I was a lad growing up in Brooklyn there was only cricket. Now it is different. But you can blame whatever you want for the poor and declining standards – too much money, one-day cricket and the subsequent denigration of Tests – but in the end there is only one logical cause, and that is a lack of talent. The Aussies missed Greg Chappell, perhaps more than they realised.

Another Australian, the leg spinner Kerry O'Keeffe, replaced Chappell at Somerset for a couple of, as it turned out, unproductive years. O'Keeffe came from New South Wales and went on to play for his country, but he never got the hang of the demands of the county game. I recall having a conversation with him and we got talking about the Australians visit to England the next year, 1972. I told him I thought England would win the series. He looked at me hard. "You know what your trouble is," he said, "You have been in this country too long". He hit the nail on the head. My loyalties were now well and truly divided. As an umpire, I looked upon his comment as a compliment.

10
More Controversy

I WAS RE-APPOINTED to the Test panel for 1976 and stood at both Old Trafford and the Oval when the West Indies began their total domination of the world game by winning the series 3-0. At this stage of my career I felt completely at ease umpiring at the highest level, and I was both delighted and flattered to get the nod again for the 1977 season when the Australians were due once more, this time for a full series of five Tests.

After the unsavoury experience of Lord's two years before, I was looking forward to being involved again, if only to lay that particular ghost. In the intervening two years the Chappell Affair had troubled me and I can't say that I was sorry to hear he had retired in the meantime and that his brother was now leading the side. Even so, you can imagine my anxiety when I was chosen to stand at Old Trafford for the Second Test after the first, at Lord's, had been drawn.

I am pleased to say the match at Old Trafford passed off without any extraordinary incidents. Doug Walters made 88 in an Australian total of 297, but without Dennis Lillee they struggled to contain England. With Bob Woolmer scoring 137, England ended their first innings a healthy 140 ahead. When the Aussies batted again Greg Chappell showed his quality with a fighting 112, but Derek Underwood came into his own and, by taking six wickets for 66, set up a comfortable and comprehensive nine wicket win for his country.

After the hot-house conditions of Lord's two years previously, I had expected it all to be a little fiercer, particularly as Thomson and Max Walker were still operating for Australia and Greig was firmly entrenched in the England team, albeit under Brearley's leadership. But it was not, and with England winning the next Test, at Trent Bridge, by an equally decisive margin of seven wickets, I anticipated the Fourth Test at Headingley with some relish when I was asked to be one of the umpires. Little did I realise that I was about to run into controversy once again; this time big enough to bring a temporary halt to my life as a Test umpire.

It all centred around Geoff Boycott, a man by no means foreign to a bit of controversy himself, but I hasten to add that on this occasion, while he was a key figure in the episode I'm convinced finished me, he was not to blame. I look back on England versus Australia at Headingley as one of the most disastrous of my era, but in retrospect I must again accuse the Australians of failing to accept decisions that go against them with a proper grace and sportsmanship. Needless to say, it was one of my decisions which caused a storm.

Headingley was packed that first morning, filled to the rafters with Yorkshiremen anticipating the 100th first-class century of their great hero, Boycott. Geoffrey was no fool. Here was the perfect occasion and the perfect platform. All he had to do was deliver the goods and he could have had the freedom of his entire native county. Sure enough, England batted first and the crowd sat back and waited. Imagine their delight when Brearley, the personification of everything they disliked about the south of England, was caught behind off Thomson without a run on the board. Geoff dug in and the combined efforts of Thommo, Walker and Len Pascoe never looked like disturbing his serene and stately progress towards the inevitable. Bob Woolmer and Derek Randall each made useful scores as the Australian attack began to wane and flounder against Boycott's dead bat.

It was when Tony Greig came to the crease, and with the Australians growing more desperate by the minute, that the whole match blew apart. By now Boycott was well on his way and the crowd were beginning to sense that history was about to be made in front of their very eyes. Pro-Boycott banners sprouted from the terracing and, spurred on by liberal helpings of the local brew, the Yorkshiremen began to applaud every flick, nudge and push as

111

Boycott's score mounted run by run. I think the Aussies may have been a little rattled by all this because their agitation was plain for all to see. Australians love a good challenge, and they did not come any greater than to remove Boycott before he had reached his ton and to spoil the party by ramming the chants and songs of the partisan support right back down their throats.

Boycott hardly gave a glimmer of a chance as Greg Chappell turned to the left arm spin of Ray Bright in another attempt to make a breakthrough. I was standing at the bowler's end when Bright wheeled in once more to Boycott, then on 75, with the wicket-keeper Rod Marsh standing up to the slower bowling. The ball was going down the leg-side and Boycott, without trying an extravagant sweep or anything definite, looked as if he was merely attempting to help the ball on its way. Boycott flailed away and Marsh held it. The next thing I knew the Australians were roaring for a catch. Not surprisingly, Boycott did not move a muscle. It was up to me to make a decision. "Not out", I said. The crowd, for once silenced by the appeal and a rare sign of fallibility from "The Master", were quick to show their relief. But the Aussies just could not believe my verdict. They went mad; absolutely berserk. For a terrible moment I thought I had a full scale riot on my hands as the Australian fielders lost all control of themselves. I was in deep trouble once again.

Bright was adamant Boycott was out and stood there defying me not to change my mind. His teammates could not contain their disbelief and anger. I have never heard such a tirade of abuse levelled at me, Boycott and everyone else as the whole fielding side swore and cursed the very ground they stood on. It was my turn to be rattled. There was no chance of the game continuing as the foul language and open dissent grew more intense and personal.

My control and calm was further undermined by Greig, standing next to me at the non-striker's end. Greig obviously could not understand my decision either. He gave me the most incredible look, shaking his head slowly from side to side as if he, too, thought I had made a bad mistake. I realised Greig and Boycott were a million miles apart in their cricket thinking and I knew also that they were never the best of friends, to put it mildly. But I never thought I would see the day when one batsman all but said his batting partner should have been given out. I was left in no doubt that Greig was convinced I should have sent Boycott packing and I was shocked to witness his antics as he grimaced and muttered while all around him his greatest opponents raged on and on. Bright snatched his cap and David Hookes, fielding at cover, was beside himself with anger and astonishment. Had he been on a football field, the referee would have sent him off for persistent dissent. He would not shut up.

As the tumult showed no signs of dying I made my way over to Hookes to give him a lecture. I told him, as one Australian to another, that I would have no hesitation in dismissing him from the field. I warned him that I could not tolerate such open questioning of my authority. I had made my decision, I said to him, and he must accept it. From cover point there was no way he could have had a better view of a catch down the leg-side and I added that if he did not like it he could leave the field, pack his bags and head home. As Hookes stood there, hands on hips, Chappell came over to sort it out. "Greg," I said, "Unless you tell your men to shut up immediately this game will not restart". Greg realised it had all gone too far. "Cool it Hookesy," he told him. Then he went back to the slips delivering his orders to calm down as he went.

After what had seemed like an eternity, we were able to start once more. The madness may have calmed but the controversy had not. This was my last Test match for three years and I am utterly convinced that this one incident was the reason I was demoted from the Test panel at the end of the summer. By giving Boycott not out, I had signed my own death warrant.

Australians still talk about this one incident now. Their cricketers that day claimed that in trying to turn the ball around the corner, it had brushed Boycott's glove and Marsh had held a legitimate catch. There was no nick from the bat, so that had Boycott been out the ball must have struck the glove. I have watched numerous replays of the delivery since that fateful day and I am sure I was correct in making the decision that I did. I defy any umpire standing from where I was standing to have given Boycott out. My vision was obscured by his body as he swung around. Anything could have happened. I admit I could have been wrong, but I will say to my dying day that no umpire could have given a categorical "yes" to that appeal. The batsman has the benefit of any doubt and in this case there was a massive amount of doubt. An umpire must be sure a batsman is out before he raises his finger. While I concede Boycott might well have been out, I could not be certain and, because I was not one hundred per cent positive, I gave him the benefit of that doubt. I believe that no first class umpire, in my position, would have made a different decision. As I discovered at Lord's two years before, the Australians will appeal for anything. If I gave a batsman out for every such query, a Test would not go into a second day.

Curiously, I felt I had made a good job of bringing the Australian fielders back to earth after their fury had threatened to bring the game to a grinding halt. Chappell had acted sensibly, admonished Hookes and restored peace around the rest of his field. I had not lost control and I did not think I was as shaken as I had been at Lord's. Obviously, I had not expected Boycott to tuck his bat under his arm and head for the pavilion, but I was intrigued by the reaction of Marsh. He appealed initially – as he always did – but thereafter he remained noticeably calmer than his hysterical colleagues. Did he know something the others did not? What I must own up to was my own reaction to Hookes's bad-mouthing at cover point. I was as angered by his dissent as he was by my decision and, for two or three minutes while I delivered my lecture, I came fairly close to doing something I would have regretted for the rest of my life. I am sure that had he not shut up when I told him to, I would have struck him, though I like to think good sense would have prevailed. I liked a fight when I was younger and I was very annoyed by his attitude. None of his abuse, from what I could make out, was directed specifically at me but I will never understand how a cricketer could have behaved the way he did.

When play resumed at long last, the atmosphere was terrible. The Australians carried on in silence. They were already two down in the series and their heart had gone. To the increasing delight of his multitude of supporters, Boycott dug in once more and ground inexorably towards the century he had set his heart on.

Eventually it came. Without the slightest hint of nerves, Boycott reached his ton and Headingley erupted. Banners waved, people were openly crying and the great man acknowledged it all as he had done 99 times before, by raising his bat aloft. Chappell and one or two of his teammates put their hands together in polite applause. Most of the team stood stonily unemotional, reflecting on what might have been. Their refusal to join in the celebrations spoke more eloquently than a thousand words. Quite plainly, they were disgusted. Boycott ignored their protests, silent though they were by now, and got his revenge as only he could. With his century under his belt, Boycott simply took his guard again and settled down to grind his opponents into the Headingley turf. By the time Pascoe had him caught, Boycott had made 191 and England had achieved a thoroughly solid 436.

The Australians had been beaten into submission by him and, when it was their turn to bat, it seemed obvious to me that they had no stomach for what remained of the contest. Ian Botham, with five wickets, and Mike Hendrick with four more, ripped through them and they were all out for 103. Made to follow on, they played a little better second time around but were all out for 248, giving their oldest rivals their third win of the series, by an innings and 85 runs. From my point of view, the rest of the match passed off without incident on the field but the whole affair had been marred by what had happened on that first day.

I will admit now that I went out that first morning scarcely in the best frame of mind, although in my own defence I must say that how I felt had no bearing on my decision not to give Boycott out. Before the start it became known that the England players had each been given £1,000 by a window cleaning company director. It was a generous gesture by a supporter and the England players were duly grateful. But his benevolence did not please me. I felt the umpires had once more been overlooked. I have never undersold myself as a cricketer or an umpire and I felt we should have been on the receiving end of some of this generosity. Umpires have not always been treated as well as they might over the years and it annoyed me that, with all this money flying about, Lloyd Budd and myself were not getting any of it. I said as much to several prominent people within the game at the time. I was not saying we should have received an equal amount, but I did think our part in the proceedings should have been recognised. Budd was a gentle sort of character and he thought the benefactor could do what he liked with his money, but it was the principle of the matter which so irritated me.

Anyway, despite my protests before the start of play, we never did get our money and I made my way out to the field of play rather less than filled with the joys of summer. At the end of the day, of course, I was even more unhappy, with an outsize controversy hanging over my head. Peter Lush, the public relations man at Lord's, could see the Boycott incident was a heaven-sent story for the newspapers and he was quickly into the umpires' room at the end of play. Whatever you do, he told me, say nothing to the Press. I agreed to his request, but I would have liked to have been able to put over my side of the story.

Needless to say, Boycott was the hero of the hour and all the publicity centred around his achievement. But the ill-feeling lingered. Len Maddocks, the Australian manager, could not hide his feelings. Budd and me brought the players off the field a few minutes early during the same match because of bad light. The light was not getting any better and as far as we were concerned it was not good enough to resume before the scheduled close. We began to undress and unwind. I was quietly minding my own business when Maddocks stuck his head around the door. "I thought it courtesy to tell the touring captain that play was off for the day," he said. I apologised but I pointed out to him that it should have all seemed fairly obvious bearing in mind the quality of the light.

Maddocks did not stop to hear my explanation. Budd, a former policeman who came into the game late in life, was worried by Maddocks' tone. He left the room determined to make amends, albeit belatedly. He went into the Australian dressing-room and told Chappell formally that play was over for the day. Chappell acknowledged him but did not lift his eyes from the floor.

That night we were invited to attend a cocktail party at which the players of both sides were also guests. I can honestly say that no one spoke to us when we got there. It would have been apparent to all but the most thick-skinned that we were not welcome. Budd and I knocked back our drinks and left as quietly as we came. "I don't think they want us here," I told Budd as we left the room. Test matches are not social matches. No one needs to tell me that. But it seems the Boycott decision and then our failure to tell the Australians about the end of play had conspired to get me ostracised. If I was being ostracised because I was only doing my job, then I have no regrets. Even today, I cannot believe Maddocks and Chappell were really upset about our inability to tell them formally that play was off, but it gave them an excuse – and that I do regret.

I believe this final controversy was the reason I was dropped from the Test panel for the following year. Just before the start of the 1978 season I got a call from Lord's to tell me I had not been re-selected. I dropped the phone in sheer, utter amazement. I simply could not believe it. It was like a bad dream. I staggered into my sitting-room rendered speechless by the news. To say that I was desperately shocked would have been an understatement. I was livid, hurt and deeply wounded all at the same time.

When the initial sensation wore off I started to think why and where I had gone wrong. Lord's were not obliged to offer me an explanation and they certainly didn't offer one. I had given them four years loyal and honest service in seven Tests and now I was gone without so much as a thank-you. My sacking – and there was no other word for it – had come right out of the blue. I took it all very badly, brooding for days over my dismissal and coming, no matter in which directions my thoughts went, back to the same conclusion. The Australian management had obviously made it plain that they were unhappy with my umpiring. Whether or not this was a legacy of the series in 1975, I shall never know. Nor will I ever know if Len Maddocks had issued a formal complaint about that one particular incident involving Boycott, or about my methods in general. I cannot even be sure that Maddocks made any complaint at all. I may be maligning him unnecessarily, but I feel sure this was the reason I was not retained for another year.

Even now I have no real knowledge why I was taken off the list. I only got on the panel in the first place because I was known to be and seen to be a strong umpire. I cannot believe I let anyone down on that score while I was standing in Test matches. England against Australia is no occasion for a novice player or umpire. I stood firm under the sort of provocation which would have finished men with more fragile temperaments. These sort of matches call for men who will not be intimidated under any circumstances, and never once did I buckle. When I think of some of the men umpiring county matches I wonder what on earth they would have done faced with the sort of hostility I met at Headingley. No one said a word of criticism to me during that match, nor during the rest of the season. I received no adverse reports and no letter to say where I had erred, if at all. A quiet word might have saved me a lot of suffering. Everyone makes mistakes. I only wish I had been told what mine had been.

The papers rang to get my comments on my demotion. I had to bite my tongue. I could say nothing of any consequence but I am equally sure my hurt was obvious to all. What made it worse was that I could not go on record about why I thought I had been sacked. I would have loved to have got in touch with Mr. Maddocks and told him I was simply doing my job to the best of my ability.

My old Somerset teammate Ken Palmer was nominated to replace me and for all my hurt pride I was pleased for him. He was far younger than me and had proved himself on the county circuit to be reliable and thoroughly diligent. Perhaps the powers at Lord's thought it time to promote him to the Test panel, and I, at 59, was the man to make way for him. I only wish I had been told as much. However, this theory, comforting though it may have been to me, went out of the window two years later when I was re-appointed four years short of my old age pension. Hard as I looked for other reasons, I was left with the only real cause for my absence from the 1978 Test panel. It was simply that my work had brought complaints at the highest level and, as a sop to Anglo-Australian relations, I had been put out to grass. I was sentenced to two years non-stop county cricket and, apart from resigning, I had no alternative but to grin and bear it. Of course, everywhere I went I was asked why I was no longer a Test match umpire. I could give them no straight answer and, even if I had known, I was bound by my contract to say nothing.

Gradually I shrugged off the disappointment and my love for the game overcame the crippling blow to my morale. I was among the first to congratulate Palmer on his elevation and he went on to achieve a deserved reputation as one of the best officials in international cricket. I did not find it difficult to offer him my best wishes because I genuinely wanted him to be a success.

The same could not be said for Dusty Rhodes when I first became a Test umpire at his expense. Dusty had been an outstanding umpire in his heyday, and, like me, took it badly when he was taken off the panel. In effect, it was his job I took when I stepped up in 1974. We were listed to officiate at a Lancashire match at Old Trafford against Pakistan soon after the announcement that I had replaced him on the Test panel. In such circumstances the two umpires, thrust together for three days, have to be close allies, friends and confidants, even though you may not see each other again for another three months. But poor old Dusty took it as a personal insult and ignored me for the entire duration of the match, as if he had fallen victim to a plot instigated by me. For three days he did not so much as wish me a good morning. Every time I attempted to explain to him that it was none of my doing he shuffled away, obviously still deeply hurt and unhappy. Dusty never did get back on the Test panel, but I only wish he had realised I was as surprised as he was about my rise to prominence. For that reason I was quick to offer my best wishes to Palmer. He had earned his chance and now it was up to me to get back.

For two years I was left to replay the Boycott incident over and over again in my mind, convinced as I was that this one ball was the root cause of my dismissal. Time after time I came back to the same conclusion. I could not and did not dispute that Boycott may have touched the delivery, either with his bat or, more likely, with his glove. My only defence is that from my position I did not see him do it and for that reason I could not give him out.

During my two years of penance my emotions changed slightly. My grief subsided and it was replaced by a constant feeling of mystification. Many of life's problems, real or imagined, boil down to a lack of understanding. People develop a chip on their shoulder because something has not been explained to them properly - and not necessarily out of malice. I just wish someone at Lord's had had the courage, or sense of responsibility, to drop me a line to tell me why I was not a Test umpire any longer. It would have saved me and my family some heartache, and at least I would have then known where I had gone wrong. Perhaps I am naive, but it brings me back to my old theme. Umpires are given marks by team captains and they may never know why they are failing or where they are erring.

Everyone wants to do well in their job and umpires are not exceptions. We are big enough to take advice and criticism. Indeed, I am sure I speak for every umpire in England and abroad when I say that we would welcome greater consultation with players and the game's officials. I suppose we are like football referees in that we are taken for granted more often than not, and yet the game could not go ahead without us. They say the best referees are the ones who are never noticed during a match. Cricket umpires have to be far more ostentatious but the principles are the same.

As it was, in the absence of any official explanation I was left to make my own deductions. Simply, they were that by not giving out one batsman I had given myself out of Test cricket. An over-simplification maybe, but in all honesty I can think of no other excuse. I returned to county cricket a sadder and wiser man, determined to prove I was still worthy to be ranked among the best in the business, but I did so with a heavy heart.

11
Lord's 1974 and its aftermath

ONE OF MY biggest regrets was only ever being asked to umpire in one major cup final at Lord's. In 1974, the year I started on the Test panel, I was chosen to stand with Dickie Bird in the Benson and Hedges final between Surrey and Leicestershire, but as usual the match was not without incident as far as I was concerned - and it was pointedly my last big domestic final. Once more, I am afraid to admit, my actions during a match moved one party to complain and for the last ten years of my career I was made to pay for giving what I will always believe were honest decisions.

I have often been asked what my ambitions were as an umpire and I used to reply, tongue in cheek, that before I retired I wanted to give all ten batsmen out leg before wicket. I gave three against Leicestershire and, with one of them particularly contentious, I never got another chance to stand in a Lord's showpiece. Cup finals at Lord's are always magnificent occasions, as I discovered as a Somerset player in 1967. The famous ground is always packed with supporters of both sides and the presence of national television puts ordinary county players into the spotlight, very often for the only time in their careers.

Surrey and Leicestershire both had a smattering of Test calibre players who had tasted life as international cricketers, but there were others for whom this was their big day. I saw my own selection as confirmation of my growing reputation as one of the firmest umpires in the country and, having become a Test umpire in the same season, my progress was seen to be fairly rapid.

As usual Lord's was full and I had every reason to look forward to the day ahead. I knew all the players on first name terms, was well aware of any potential trouble-makers, and, even allowing for the gravity of a big match, had every right to expect a day to be enjoyed.

It all began innocently enough with John Edrich, the Surrey skipper, winning the toss and deciding to bat first. Edrich was obliged to defend for long periods against the wily bowling of Ken Higgs, the experienced former England player, and it was obvious from the start from the way the wicket was playing that it would be a low-scoring affair. I gave out Edrich's opening partner, Lonsdale Skinner, leg before without scoring, the first of what one critic wrote were: "four death-dealing instances in response to lbw shouts". The same critic said Bill Alley "donned his black hat that day". I can only say that it turned out to be my funeral.

Edrich grafted away in that gutsy, tenacious way of his, scoring 40 in 36 overs, which included, so the record book says, 18 in 24 overs. Younis Ahmed livened the run rate with a brisk 43 and, in a late burst, Robin Jackman contributed some big-hitting in his innings of 36, which helped Surrey reach a respectable but by no means match-winning 170. Higgs was particularly difficult to get away that day, taking four wickets for ten runs in seven tight and economical overs. His figures were enhanced by a hat-trick. He removed Alan Butcher and Pat Pocock, and then, with the focus of a cricketing nation centred on his next ball, he bowled Arnold Long.

As we left the field at the end of the Surrey innings, the Leicestershire players and supporters had every reason to feel satisfied with the way the match was going. From their point of view, it was there for the taking. Apart from giving out poor old Skinner before he had scored, the first half of the match had passed without memorable incident and I was anticipating the Leicestershire reply with as much relish as their supporters.

Leicestershire were being led by Ray Illingworth, who since his exile from Yorkshire had built up a good all-round team and, for the first time in the history of the club, were about to start winning a few trophies. For more years than they care to remember they were the poor relations of county cricket, but, like Somerset, had, through careful planning, assembled a team and an organisation fit to rival bigger and better equipped counties. Even so, this was only the second major final in Leicestershire's history, and I suspect the occasion meant rather more to them as a county than to their opponents, who had always been a major power for as long as I had been in England, and before.

To overhaul Surrey's modest total, Leicestershire needed to make a steady start, but that's where I came into it. Geoff Arnold bowled the first ball of the Leicestershire innings and, as he rapped Barry Dudleston on the pads, shouted one of those stentorian appeals of his to which I had no hesitation in agreeing. Dudleston did not look happy, but he had only himself to blame, and the ignominy of getting out first ball, I believe, had much to do with his sorrowful expression as he made the long walk to the pavilion he had only recently left.

The Leicestershire fans were obviously upset at such a setback, but Maurice Norman and the obdurate figure of John Steele started to repair the damage with a valuable second wicket partnership of 46, which appeared to put Leicestershire back into a winning position. Then Graham Roope, the Surrey bowler, appealed for leg before against Norman and, once more, I had no doubts he was a "goner". The Leicestershire fans, with the drink now doing its share of the talking, had begun to identify me as the villain of the piece. Two wickets down and Bill Alley was responsible for both.

When Steele was run out in a muddle with Brian Davison, the game was beginning to slip away from Leicestershire and how Davison and Roger Tolchard were able to cope as the fourth wicket pair was crucial to the whole proceedings. Tolchard went on to play a few games for England as a wicketkeeper-batsman, but he will be best remembered as a great exponent of limited-overs cricket. His running between the wickets was always a treat to watch, and his ability to get runs in situations as tight as this was a key factor in Leicestershire's subsequent success under Illingworth. At 46 for three, Tolchard figured he needed to get a sight of the bowling before he attempted to attack it. Roope was still wheeling away with his restrictive medium-paced bowling and Tolchard decided the best way to counter it was to pad-up without offering a shot.

124

It is a dangerous ploy at the best of times and Roope more than once made polite inquiries for leg before. I gave the matter due consideration before rejecting the appeals, but I was the first to concede there was not much in it. Roope was getting close but Tolchard failed to sense his spoiling tactics might be near to rebounding on him.

Eventually, it had to happen. Roope again struck Tolchard's pads, pushed down the wicket as they were. I was convinced he was not offering a shot. This time I had no hesitation. "That's out," I said, raising my finger. Tolchard could not believe it. His disagreement was fairly obvious as he trudged back with Leicestershire now poised at 50 for four, and a long way from victory. Tolchard and his county were later to contend that he had proffered a shot as he lunged forward with pad and bat. I was not having any of it. To this day I cannot believe his "shot" was a genuine attempt to play the ball, and I lost no sleep over giving him out.

Leicestershire never recovered. Davison, who was a magnificent stroke-maker, was caught in the covers, and although the reliable Chris Balderstone grafted away for 32 precious runs, it was only delaying the inevitable. Arnold finished with three for 20, Pocock took three for 26 and Roope's accuracy was rewarded with figures of two for 30. Leicestershire quietly subsided and they were all out for 143 to give Surrey the cup by a margin of 27 runs, which was rather more comprehensive than the score would suggest.

The finale was all rather muted, but I was totally unprepared for the reception which greeted me as I left the field. While Surrey supporters acclaimed their heroes, the Leicestershire fans decided their defeat was my fault. A crescendo of booing percolated through the applause for Surrey and a little ripple of chanting, "Alley out", grew in intensity - to my utter surprise and horror! Surely they were not blaming me?

Unfortunately, they most certainly were laying the blame firmly and squarely at my feet. The hostility of the losing supporters was even more evident when the awards ceremony took place soon afterwards. Some of the more incensed among them started hurling the occasional drink-inspired insult in my direction. I endeavoured to keep my calm and self-control as the match adjudicator, Freddie Brown, decided Edrich's contribution in runs and shrewd captaincy was enough to earn him the Gold Award for man-of-the-match.

I must admit I did not think too much more of it. Of course, the Leicestershire backing were disappointed. They had come a long way and had seen their team beaten without really making much of a contest of it. In such circumstances it is easy to look for, and find, a scapegoat. That day it was my turn; I was one of the men who had to make decisions and it was me who they turned into the scapegoat. I stayed for a drink or two after the game, had a little chat with the players of both sides without noticing anything untoward, and departed with a clear conscience, convinced in my own mind that every judgement I had made had been correct.

The sequel to all this came a day or two later when I got a call from a man in a prominent position at Lord's, the secretary of the TCCB, Donald Carr. He had noticed from the fixture list that I was down to umpire at Leicestershire in a John Player League match only eight days after their appearance in the Benson and Hedges Cup final at Lord's. He suggested to me that I should either swap with another umpire or simply not go to Leicester. It was apparent to me straight away that there had been some manoeuvring behind the scenes. In short, there had been complaints about the way I had handled the final. I could understand that in the heat of the moment at the end of a losing final words might have been said, but it struck me something more formal had taken place. I know Donald only had my interests at heart. He realised the depth of feeling in the Leicestershire camp against me, and he knew that by fulfilling the obligation just over a week later I was letting myself in for quite a day. But I was adamant. I was not going to be intimidated by people who had not even had the courage to confront me, face to face, man to man, with their grudge. I was not going to give way. My reply could not have been straighter. "I do that match or I quit the game," I told the secretary.

In fairness, he was giving me the chance to back out, but when he heard my feelings he did not pursue the matter. "All right," he said. "It's up to you – and the best of luck". I was furious. It wasn't the suggestion that I should do something else that Sunday which made me so livid as the thought that, behind my back, Leicestershire had registered their disapproval of my umpiring, and this was the only way I would have found out about it. I could hardly comprehend that they had identified me as the reason for their failure to win the match. I went up to Grace Road eight days later determined to stand my ground and defend my reputation.

Leicestershire have what they call their 100 Club, and it was they who provided a pretty warm reception for me when I reached their ground for the Sunday match with Yorkshire. As the umpires came out before the start of play I was roundly booed and derided. I just stuck my Australian jaw out a little further and got on with the business of the day. The same happened at the tea interval and again at the close of play. I had expected it and I can honestly say I was not worried by it, merely perplexed that they still believed, eight days on, that their defeat at Lord's was all down to me. I had expected such treatment from the supporters with the members of their fanatical 100 Club giving me all they had got. What I had not anticipated was the cold-shoulder I received off the field from the normally friendly staff and officials!

Ironically, Leicestershire had always been one of the most hospitable clubs on the county circuit. Mike Turner, the secretary-manager, had quietly worked a miracle with limited resources. Leicestershire had never chased any honours, nor had they ever been embarrassed by an over-abundance of talent, but before Turner began his revolution, they had rightfully earned a reputation for their friendliness, courtesy and good humour. Mike Turner could not have been nicer to me over the years. He always made sure I had a drink with him at the end of a day's play and I never went there when they did not offer red wine with my lunch. I enjoyed going to Grace Road and so did other umpires. But their cheeriness disappeared overnight. One minute I was an Australian character, the next I was a foreign rogue. The hospitality dried up instantly. There were no more post-match drinks with the committee, and the lunchtime red wine became a thing of the past.

I was surprised and taken aback, but I thought to myself that, though they were being a little childish, their reaction was at least understandable so soon after the Lord's debacle. That particular day no one from Leicestershire, players or officials, so much as bothered to pass the time of day with me. I did not cry over my sudden casting out. I laughed at the supporters who booed me. The more they did it, the more I lapped it up. I told them I would write about them one day in a book and now I have. Off the field it was rather more difficult to take, especially from people whom I had considered were friends. The players, again naturally enough, did not want to know me. When they were fielding none of them spoke to me, but you could cut the atmosphere with a knife. It was altogether an unpleasant day, but I knew I had to go through with it, and in a perverse way I was glad I did. I was well aware it was going to be an ordeal, and it had been. Nevertheless, I had come through it with my head held high and I had every reason to expect relations to return to normal the following season, at the very latest.

How wrong I was. My punishment was to continue for ten years until I retired from the game. Leicestershire, I believe, never fully forgave me for what they had considered were my errors that day at Lord's in 1974. Looking back on it, I wonder who it was that had complained about me and on what score. Illingworth could be a little hot-headed at times, if things were going against him or his team. I cannot, though, believe, even now, that he made a protest of any kind. The legacy of what turned out to be my only final was to haunt me for ten painful years. Illingworth's players were fiercely loyal to him and, all the while they continued to play for Leicestershire, I came to realise that I was never again going to be readmitted to their confidence and become friends once more. Our relationship was never repaired and it was always a source of regret that we were never able to make it up.

Towards the end of my time, the last of Illy's team had gone, and it was easier to talk to the younger lads for whom that particular final was only a piece of history. They bore no grudge, but I am sure many of the 1974 team went into retirement with a sense of grievance about me. I never did get my red wine at lunch-times. They were a luxury of the past and I was never a guest again of Mike Turner and the committee. We were on speaking terms by the end, I am pleased to report, but the old sense of bonhomie had long gone. Even in my last season there was still a lingering resentment, most notably from the Leicestershire supporters.

There is nothing more I would have liked than to have gone out universally loved and admired. I suppose it was too much to ask. As I shall reveal later, most of the counties provided the most welcome selection of presents any man could wish for. There had to be one county who didn't get along with me. It must be the same with other umpires. In my case the good feeling generated by Essex and many other clubs was always contrasted by Leicestershire, and it will always be a source of deep regret that we parted on rather less than the best of terms.

Unfortunately, the nastiness which surrounded my first final had much to do with it being my last. For all the controversy, I thoroughly enjoyed the final and, since I had only that year been put onto the Test panel, I was confidently looking forward to several more. It was not an unreasonable expectation in the circumstances. I have to be philosophical about it. Many umpires never get the chance to stand in a Lord's final. At least I had the honour of doing one, but I would have loved to have done more. Umpires can never win and in this particular sphere I was definitely a loser.

The pressure to win matches, particularly limited overs matches, has increased over the years because of the large amounts of money available to the winners. On that point alone, it was little wonder Leicestershire were so sore. In my opinion, Kerry Packer has a lot to answer for. By putting the money in, he inadvertently took away much of the enjoyment derived by professional players and umpires. Now, because there is so much at stake, counties are in the market for the best players and they don't care where they come from. Only Yorkshire, at the time of my retirement, insisted their players were born within the Broad Acres, but it is the biggest geographical county in England, with several major cities in which to comb for talent. It is a different matter for other counties. Their horizons know no bounds. They are more likely to have a scout in the Caribbean than in some far flung outpost of their own area. Who can blame them? Certainly not me. Overseas players have saved county cricket from dying on its feet, and I am not just saying that because, in effect, I was an overseas player myself.

I cannot believe my ears when I hear distinguished people within the English game calling for a reduction - or even a ban - on players from abroad, as if that in itself would remedy the lack of genuine top-class native players. I have stood as an umpire at more deserted county grounds for more years than I care to remember, and it strikes me that what few people have bothered to turn up have come to see the big name overseas players perform, not some county trundler. I say categorically that, for the sake of English cricket, the overseas players must be encouraged to stay, and if I was running a county I would be looking to bring in even more. It costs a lot of money to step inside a county ground for a day's play. Believe me, no one is going to pay that sort of money to watch ordinary players no matter where they were born. Spectators want to see the best and, as opposed to 30 years ago, have now come to expect it.

Cricket is a business nowadays and unless they provide the best possible fare then the public will simply find something else to do. The leisure industry had provided many appealing alternatives in the last few years and no one has to go to a cricket ground, with their hard seats and poor facilities, for entertainment. I would like to see a far greater turnover of players. I am not advocating a football-style transfer system, but I believe some players stay with a county for too long. Crowds get sick of seeing the same mediocre players performing, scraping together 1,000 runs in a county season, or picking up the occasional wicket here and there in a slog. Nobody wants to see them for any longer than it takes to find out if they are going to make the grade. Counties are not ruthless enough with these guys. Three years and they should be gone if they aren't going to be any real value other than to occupy a batting space.

In England the benefit system, whereby capped players have a year in which to make a pile of tax-free money, has prevented a freer flowing system of players. In Australia there is a far greater turnover within the states. It is rare over there to find a player aged 30 still playing Sheffield Shield cricket who either has not been or is still a candidate for a Test place. Lesser players would have given up somewhere along the line when it became obvious they were not going to be stars and dropped out of first-class cricket to concentrate on another career, just playing at the weekends for relaxation. In England the counties are clogged with ordinary lads hanging on for their benefits and, in the process, contributing virtually nothing. Promising schoolboys contemplating a career in professional cricket must despair when they see the same old names, year after year, blocking the way. Fresh faces stimulate the public and stimulate the game. I say keep the overseas players and get shot of some of the game's many nonentities. I would like to see a benefit being awarded after five years instead of ten and then players should be moved out unless, of course, they were exceptional. New faces and a constant stream of top-class overseas players will keep the clubs strong.

It occurs to me that those in the game looking at its best interests are going about reforms in the wrong way, and the reduction of overseas players will take its toll at the turnstiles and not necessarily open the way for bright local talent. To the game's administrators, I say think again.

I cannot believe either that the lack of discipline within the game these days does anything for the game's image, or for the number of people paying at the gate. I am always impressed by the way the Sri Lankans, the Indians, the Pakistanis and the West Indies deport themselves when they come to England. They realise they are representing their countries and act and dress accordingly in collar, tie and blazers. But the Australians on tour make me wince with embarrassment at times. More often than not when they are not on the field of play they can be spotted in T-shirts, dirty shorts and sandals. They behave like children in half-grown beards, wandering around with head-phones pinned to their ears in a sloppy little world of their own. They are a poor advertisement for their country when they come to England, and I dare say they behave in much the same way elsewhere. If Australian supporters could see these heroes abroad they would share my disgust and concern. It strikes me that they simply don't care what image they portray.

Not that players in England are any better. Over the years I have noticed, with a certain amount of horror, the deteriorating standards in dress, behaviour and attitude to their job. Roger Knight, a schoolmaster by profession and for many years the respected captain of Surrey, had the right idea. He insisted his players wore the club blazer and jeans were strictly frowned upon. As an umpire it was not uncommon to have a bowler's cap or sweater flung at me as if I was some skivvy. One lad threw me his cap and it landed short. "My cap's on the ground," he shouted as he ran back to his fielding position. "And that's where it will stay, son," I told him, "Unless you pick it up and give it to me properly". It was the only way to deal with these scruffy little kids.

What concerned me almost as much was the way the players – and I am talking about paid county players – treated their own gear. I remember one bowler handing me his sweater and I could smell it from five yards away. To spare his blushes I won't actually name the culprit, other than to say he became an administrator within the game, but I was astonished that he had obviously not washed his county jumper all summer. I took an instant dislike to this sweater. "I am not even going to touch this," I informed the rather surprised owner. Shamefacedly he took it back without so much as a murmur of protest. He knew he was guilty.

Lancashire, I am told, even went so far as to cut out girlie magazines from the dressing-room in a bid to tighten discipline. I suppose coaching and leadership have much to do with the type of players being turned out. In my last years as an umpire all I saw were teams of children. Because of a desperate lack of quality, many young lads are getting a chance now when they are hardly ready. I am forced to come to the conclusion that the general standard of cricketer, around the globe, is not as good as it was. There are plenty of coaches and plenty of coaching. So why are standards not higher? I can only assume the wrong type of coaching advice is being offered. Perhaps coaches are not concentrating on basics, or instilling the right things. In my opinion they could make a start on the discipline. I noticed youngsters don't talk cricket like we used to at the end of the day. It is sad to be in the bar at the end of a long day's play not to see the young lads in there tapping up the more experienced. I, for one, was always available to help, but very few players came along to ask for it. I'm not saying I had all the answers, but I had been involved in top-class cricket since before many of them were born. When I was a player we used to talk about the game and little else all night. The kids masquerading as county players today don't appear to me to have the ability to talk about it in the same depth, nor do they have the same technical knowledge. As a lover of cricket I am sorry this is the situation. For the sake of the game I love, and which has been so good to me, I hope there is soon a change for the better.

They can all learn something from Richard Hadlee, who when he first came to England from New Zealand to play for Nottinghamshire was a raw youngster who obviously felt he had a bit to prove. I told him to calm down because he was a fierce appealer, and he listened to me and asked for observations. I rated him the best of modern bowlers. He actually thanked umpires for holding his sweaters while he bowled and, when he did appeal, it was fairly certain it had to be a close decision.

For some other prominent players appealing will always be automatic rather than considered. I once had a run-in with Phil Edmonds at Lord's where he was getting the ball to bite, lift and turn with disconcerting regularity. I rate only Derek Underwood as a better left arm bowler, but on this occasion he was turning the ball too much for his own good. He must have bellowed ten or twelve appeals, but there was never any doubt in my mind that he was wasting his time. Eventually he turned and out of sheer exasperation said: "What's the bloody good? You wouldn't give him out anyway". Luckily for him, I took it as a joke and later we both laughed about the incident. Edmonds might not have been forgiven if he had used stronger language. Many other players do. I found uncapped players who were still new to the game the worst. I did not mind the occasional oath in the middle, but it used to concern me that the public would get to hear it.

As with everything on the field, it is up to the captains and the club management to set good standards, and I am sorry to report that by the time I finished there was a dearth of strong captains in county cricket; men who would be prepared to get tough on and off the field. It is the attitude of the younger element, more often than not still unproven in professional cricket, which worries me. It might seem unfair to single the boy out, but I recall a little clash with John Carr, son of Donald Carr, while he was playing for Oxford University against Kent. I saw enough of him to rate him highly as an all-rounder. On this occasion, though, he was caught, bat and pad. He refused to look in my direction. I had to give him out a second time and when I pointed this out to him he told me, "Well it's your job to give me out". I was quick to point out I had given him out, if only he had bothered to look up. This was a boy learning his cricket and yet he was trying to con me. I was very disappointed and I only hope he learnt from the incident. If there is an appeal against you, as the batsman, it concerns you and nobody else. You should respond by looking at the umpire. Many batsmen believe there is too much appealing and it is hard to disagree. It is, after all, a form of cheating and gamesmanship of any kind is to be deplored.

I find it disconcerting to see slip fielders and short-legs shouting for a catch when a batsman plays and misses. The little shout, "catch it", used to be a rarity, but now they all do it. For an experienced umpire such as I was by that time I thought it was no great worry, but younger umpires must have been put under great pressure, the more so now that there are so few good "walkers" among the world's top batsmen.

Talking of appeals reminds me of that great clown Derek Randall. Derek had just been recalled to the Test side and was playing in his last county match for Nottinghamshire before the Test. Every time a batsman played and missed the excitable Randall howled for a catch from his fielding position in the covers. No one else among the Nottinghamshire fielders was bothering. It happened time and again and I was getting fed up with it. I told his captain, Clive Rice, to tell him to shut up. Rice went over for a quiet word with him. Randall suddenly realised he was out of order and a sheepish grin played over that impish face of his. An over or two later he came over to apologise. "Sorry Bill," he said, "I was just practising for when I get back onto the Test team". That said it all!

12
Back in the Fast Lane

BY NOW you would have realised that I never knew what shock would hit me next every time I got a telephone call from Lord's. They invariably left me stunned in one way or another, and so it was again in 1980 after my two years in the county wilderness. "You're back on", I was told, "Welcome back to Test cricket".

I had no idea why I had been singled out. My marks had always been reasonable but I had not expected to return to the Test panel. I had, of course, not given up hope, but realistically I was 61 and I was certain my chance had gone. Perhaps they felt I had suffered enough. I must say I did not feel any great excitement at the news, nor any great sense of being vindicated. I knew I was one of the better umpires, so it had been up to me to prove it by consistent performances at county level. This I felt I had done. I saw it as a reward for my professionalism.

The West Indies were in England that summer and I stood in two Tests at Lord's and Headingley, both of which were drawn without ever looking like reaching a conclusion. I felt completely at ease in both and they passed off without incident. I treated them as I would have done a county match, which, since many of the West Indian players also made a living from the English domestic game, was not difficult to do. Thankfully, I did not go into either of them under any illusion that I was being scrutinised or that in some way I needed to prove myself.

I spent the winter wondering if I would get another chance to put the record straight when the Australians were due to visit England the following summer. I am pleased to say I was retained on the Test panel for 1981 and I was allocated the first Test at Trent Bridge. It was an exciting match, with England taking a narrow first innings lead of six runs but then being ripped to pieces by

Dennis Lillee and Terry Alderman, each of whom took five cheap wickets. England were all out for 125, leaving Australia 132 to win, which they only achieved with a certain amount of difficulty. At 122 for six there was even an outside chance of an England win, but the Aussies held on to go one up in the series. It all went smoothly from my point of view and I only wish I could have played a further part in what was to develop into an outstanding series dominated by the phenomenal Ian Botham. Botham was man-of-the-match in the last four Tests, three of which England won when all had seemed lost. Sadly, the Trent Bridge Test was my tenth and last. At least I had gone out on a quiet note, laying the Australian ghost once and for all in my own mind. My knees were curtailing my mobility increasingly and, in a perverse sort of way, I was not unhappy when I came off the panel for 1982. My day was over as a Test umpire and I was not unduly sorry in the circumstances.

I may have been an umpire of international repute and status, but it did not stop me having one or two more unpleasant moments, none worse than at Worcester in a match of absolutely no consequence. Worcestershire were playing a Benson and Hedges Cup group match against the traditional makeweights, the Minor Counties representative team. Dave Halfyard was the other umpire and, possibly because it was such an ordinary game, we were in a relaxed mood but, because we were professionals, I do not mean that we did not take the proceedings seriously. I admit also that it was my habit to do a lot of talking on the field, too much at times for Lord's, who in the past had told me to tone down the chat.

It's not easy to change your personality. As a player I had always been known to do my share of the laughing and joking and, while I had to respect my new position of authority, I carried on talking to all and sundry in county and Test matches once I had become an umpire. This particular match was so run-of-the-mill I can't even remember the result. A couple of days later I got a letter from Lord's reprimanding me for my behaviour. I was speechless. I thought for a moment they had got the wrong man or the wrong match. I got on to Halfyard as soon as I had recovered my senses. He had received a similar letter, berating him for not taking the match with the proper sense of gravity. Our "relaxed mood" had brought a protest from the captains, Norman Gifford of Worcestershire and Frank Collyer who was leading the Minor Counties.

I was astounded that Gifford, of all people, had either done this of his own volition or under pressure from the opposition. I had known Norman for many years. I had played against him and stood in many more matches in which he was involved. I respected him as a left-arm bowler, as a captain, as a professional cricketer and as a man. But I was shattered that he had chosen to go behind my back and report me to the game's authorities. I was made to feel like a naughty child and I felt as humiliated as Halfyard did. Gifford knew I liked a joke on the field. We had been mates and colleagues for a couple of decades and I was incensed that he had been involved in something so under-hand.

What Halfyard and I could not understand was why the captains had not approached us, either during or after the game, to register some kind of protest. That I could have understood and would have accepted. I would have been man enough to have admitted that perhaps I had been too jovial, and I am convinced I would have apologised and bought both guys a drink. I still don't know why Gifford did this and I am sad to relate we have never been able to make it up. Glenn Turner, the New Zealander who was playing for Worcestershire at the time, suggested we bury the hatchet, but we never have done. Gifford and I were still at loggerheads on the day I quit and I am afraid there is a barrier between us now which is unlikely ever to be broken down.

I suppose it is inevitable that in the best part of 40 years' professional cricket I was going to make an enemy or two along the way, but in Gifford's case it was a shame because we had been friends and I thought highly of him as a bowler. He was a little unlucky that Underwood stood in his way, barring him from all but the occasional Test appearance.

When I stepped into retirement it was sad that there were not that many outstanding bowlers in operation around the world. You would have gathered of my admiration for Hadlee. As a medium-fast bowler, I rated him the best in the world. I have watched them all from close quarters, all the big names, and Hadlee was better even than Malcolm Marshall or the other West Indians. Marshall was unquestionably the fastest but not, in my view, a more effective player in all conditions than the New Zealander.

Hadlee never gave in on any type of wicket. He would always plug away on or just outside the off-stump, varying his pace and always keeping the batsman guessing. Dennis Lillee used to say: "You never get wickets sitting in the pavilion," and he was right. I am not saying Marshall would throw in the towel when things were not running his way, but he knew when he was wasting his energy. Hadlee got results on any wicket. I think I can count on the fingers of one hand the number of deliveries I have seen him bowl down the leg-side. He moved the ball both ways with almost uncanny control and, in the days of incessant bouncers, used the short-pitched delivery as just one weapon in a considerable battery, not as his only weapon. I never saw the man in a sweat because he learned to bowl within himself, and both Nottinghamshire and New Zealand are fortunate to have had him. It would be an exaggeration to say he won Nottinghamshire the championship in 1981, but his 105 wickets at less than 15 runs each was a major factor in their triumph.

He has also brought a big up-turn in the fortunes of his country. I would go so far as to say that he put New Zealand on the cricketing map with his exploits in his career, though I have no wish to denigrate the efforts of his teammates. I am sure they would be among the first to agree. He added years to his career as Lillee, Roberts and Holding had done before him, by reducing his pace and varying it, although I think it was not until Nottinghamshire's title win that he came to be rated as highly as he deserved. He was a wiry, tough competitor and a pleasant man to umpire. He has become recognised as one of the great post-war bowlers and I often wonder what he might have achieved at international level if New

Zealand had had another bowler of similar calibre bowling from the other end. Hadlee has never been lucky enough to find someone to share his considerable work-load.

Hadlee may be the best quick bowler in recent times, but if I had to choose the best I had ever come across, I would unhesitatingly name Ray Lindwall. When I knew Ray he was something of a physical fitness fanatic who never touched a drop of drink. In his prime he seemed to live on Nestle's milk chocolate because he never seemed to eat much either. It was a positive pleasure to play in the same team because not only was he an outstanding bowler with a magnificent action, but he was also well liked. Indeed it is rare to find such a destructive cricketer of his quality so universally popular, even among his suffering opponents. I give him the edge over Lillee because he was a slightly better batsman and also because he stayed fitter throughout his career.

On the field he was a real gentleman, never moaning to his captain or to the umpires, accepting their decisions with calmness and good spirit. He was a quiet sort of man who let his cricket do his talking for him, and his career tally of 228 wickets in 61 Tests spoke eloquently enough. Like all the great men he varied his pace, mixing it up to keep a batsman on his toes and, like Hadlee and Lillee, towards the end of his career never wasted a ball. It was his faster delivery which brought him so many wickets and he only ever bowled a bouncer if he wanted to force a shot, never to intimidate. He would have considered it an utter waste of time and his carefully-conserved energy to come pounding in off that smooth run of his and then send the ball two feet over the batman's head. Had he been playing 20 years later with round-the-world television he would have made himself a fortune and earned the recognition he warranted. What is more, with so many more Tests being played now, he would have ended with many more wickets.

What I saw of Lillee over two tours I found it difficult to quite put him in the same bracket as Lindwall. He gave every umpire a hard time, but that was the way he was brought up to play cricket. I cannot think of a greater competitor on the field, though off it he and I were always good friends and I think he has a more fearsome reputation than he deserves. If I ever had cause to no-ball him he would want to know where or by how much he had strayed. I have been in the unfortunate position of having to no-ball both Gladstone Small of Warwickshire and another fine Australian bowler, Graham McKenzie, 14 times in one embarrassing over. But if it was bad for me, it was worse still for them.

Talking of the presence of television reminds me how glad umpires in England were when the habit of having a camera at square leg was abandoned. We all saw this as trial by the media and we resented it. I would go so far as to say that as many as seven out of ten close run-out decisions are the wrong ones. But in defence of the umpire I would add that with everything happening so quickly on occasion the naked eye is not fast enough to cope with all the action and be sure of making the correct verdict. Most of us would give the batsman, as always, the benefit of any doubt, but in retrospect it was all rather unsatisfactory, which is why the 1990's have seen the introduction of the third umpire and all-round television angles to judge run out decisions.

However, it will always be the job of the umpire to make other decisions in the sure knowledge that whatever he decided would be instantaneous and without prejudice. There will also always be moans from the fielding sides. This is the way it is in cricket and I only wish more players had the attitude of another great fast bowler, Wes Hall, in accepting things with a good grace. Wes was a marvellous man to play with and against. He gave everything with that perfect action of his. Roy Gilchrist and Charlie Griffiths were paired with him with varying success, but, for the most part, Wes had to carry the West Indies attack on his own – and how well he did it. I often reflect how he was able to run so far and for so long without breaking down. He was a strong man and immensely likeable.

Gilchrist was as fast a bowler as I ever faced in my career. I remember facing him at Taunton in 1957, when I opened for Somerset, and the ball flew off the bat for a couple of boundaries.

Standing the Test of Time

I can honestly say I knew next to nothing about them. I don't think I have ever been so frightened as a batsman. I used to reserve some of my best performances for the West Indies and on Gary Sober's first tour, Brian Lobb and I each took five wickets at Taunton to have them all out for 78. I must concede it would not have been so easy against the West Indian teams of the 1980's, who by allying their great talent to firm discipline, were way out in front of the other international teams. It's funny how fast bowlers carve out an impression as ogres on the field, but in the pavilion turn into the nicest men imaginable. Jeff Thomson is one such. Thommo was one of the most modest players in my experience. He was ready to talk about the game over a drink at the end of the day and, in contrast to many lesser players, never spoke about himself or his achievements. He was a pleasure to handle as an umpire. I suppose he lived in the shadow of Lillee a little, like Statham, Voce and Charlie Griffiths, suffering in comparison with their partners. I had heard he was something of a bad boy, but when he played in England for Australia and Middlesex, he was liked and respected by all he came across.

Fred Trueman was my keenest adversary when I first came into county cricket. I had some memorable clashes with Fred over the years, but although we were fierce rivals we were also great friends, bound together by mutual respect. When I started he was relying on pace alone, but as he got older he became a swing bowler and found he could be just as effective. Fred usually needed a couple of overs to warm-up and, as an opening batsman with a good eye, I found he could be a bit vulnerable until he had got into his stride. At Taunton one day he was opening the bowling for Yorkshire and I was facing him. His first ball was short and I was quickly into position to hook him for four. His next ball was a gently half-volley which I smashed back past him for four more. Fred was not a happy man. He stood scowling with his hands on his hips. "Thank you Fred," I could not resist saying. He gave me the stare. "You bastard," he retorted.

142

Back in the Fast Lane

Any success against Trueman was worth savouring but we knew we had to be at our best when we were taking him on. Peter Wight, my Somerset teammate, had some rare battles with him. In 1962, Yorkshire were staying at the County Hotel in Taunton and Fred, who liked his sleep, was not woken by his roommate, Phil Sharpe. Phil forgot to give him a nudge and Fred slept on blissfully unaware that the rest of the Yorkshire lads were on their way to the ground. When he eventually came round, Fred had to dash to the ground where he found the Yorkshire skipper, Vic Wilson, in a very unforgiving mood. Vic was something of a disciplinarian who was not prepared to tolerate such slovenliness, even from a player of Fred's reputation. Vic reprimanded him severely and then, to the surprise of us all, sent him home to Yorkshire in disgrace.

The news of Fred's banishment was quick to reach our dressing-room and we were elated by it. If we could have done, we would have gone in and given Sharpe a hug of thanksgiving. Wight could not control his happiness and burst into tears. He was crying with the simple pleasure of Fred's unseemly exit. Wiping away the tears, Peter went out and made a double century. What a way to celebrate! Mind you, Peter was just as likely to have scored those runs even if Fred had been among the opposition. The better bowlers seemed to bring out the best in him. One of his greatest combatants was Peter Loader, the Surrey and England bowler. There was always a bit of feeling between the two of them and Wight invariably came off the worst in their clashes. Fred returned time and again to haunt us and now he is one of my greatest pals. For all the controversy, which always appeared to dog his progress, he never gave less than 100 per cent for Yorkshire and England – once he had got out of bed of course!

Of all the fast bowlers I have known in recent years poor old Len Pascoe was the one for whom I felt most sympathy. Len was an aggressive bowler with a fine, fluent action, but the need to compete with Lillee, Thomson and even Rodney Hogg at their best was a little too much for him. At the top of his career Len would have been able to walk into the England team, but he made the "mistake" of being Australian. With Geoff Lawson beginning to make his mark in the same New South Wales state side, Len was under tremendous pressure just to stay in the international reckoning, and it showed on the field of play. By nature he was obviously a competitor, and he needed to be with those sort of guys. Every ball he gave the impression was going to get him a wicket and he put in everything he had got. I believe he positively hated batsmen, no matter where they came from or whom they represented. He would roar in to bowl and, with a great grunt and groan, hurl down the ball with a gusto few could match. Heaven forbid the batsman who played and missed or who got a lucky edge. Len would curse and moan at the cruel twist of fate which had somehow denied his just deserts. The batsman would be told in no uncertain terms how fortunate he had been to survive. Len liked giving the batsmen a little "chat", but there was never any sense of real malice. The crowds like to see the John McEnroes of this world and Len, without having that little something extra which would have turned him into a world-beater, was nevertheless a great-hearted trier who never gave less than his all for Australia.

But Pascoe paled into insignificance alongside the giant West Indian fast bowler Colin Croft, who, in my estimation, was the meanest of them all. When he first came to England from Guyana to play for Lancashire I had to tell him to cut out the "aggravation" because he could not differentiate between fierce commitment and over-the-top nastiness. As in most cases, you could hardly meet a nicer, more self-effacing man than Crofty in the sanctity of the dressing-room or the bar, but on the field he was a demon. To say the least, he was a difficult man to umpire because he always needed to be kept in check. If he was no-balled he could put on quite an exhibition of downright dissension. It was after one such tantrum that I warned him that if he wanted to make a name for himself as a professional cricketer, he must learn to curb his temper. He understood and, even though I am sure it had nothing to do with what I had to say, he went on to have a distinguished career with the West Indies before he ruled himself out by opting to play for the "rebels" in South Africa. But of all the West Indies hard-men, he was the one who caused umpires the greatest problems.

I suppose it takes all sorts to make a world, but his antics were always in sharp contrast to the quiet methods of Holding and Roberts, neither of whom ever gave me the slightest cause for concern. They were wonderful bowlers and had temperaments to match. Andy was a shy lad and, particularly when he first came to England, was so quiet it was a job to get a word out of him all day long. Holding never even showed the slightest hint of dissent on that occasion at Old Trafford in 1976 when I had to prevent him bowling any more short-pitched stuff at Close and Edrich. It could have been a very unpleasant incident. But because Lloyd and, more especially, Holding took my request with great dignity, it all passed off without me having to flex my muscles further. As for Roberts, it was obvious from the start that he was going to be something special. One of my first recollections of him was at Basingstoke where he proved too quick for Colin Cowdrey, and from square leg I had to give out the great man, trod on wicket.

Malcolm Marshall was about the fastest around in the mid-80's, but I do not believe he is ranked with the all-time greats. He bowls a good line and length and his sheer pace is enough to account for most of his wickets. He can get upset and, if he had a fault from the umpire's view, it is that he ran on to the wicket so much. I was forced to tell him that he would be getting an official warning after he had persistently done this, and it seemed to do the trick. Strangely, perhaps, I rated another West Indian, Sylvester Clarke of Barbados and Surrey, as a marginally better bowler. He was fast, hostile and he bowled a good line. Like Croft, he disqualified himself from the international reckoning by "defecting" to South Africa, though it was always something of a surprise to me that he had not achieved more at he highest level before doing so.

For absolute blinding pace I don't think I have ever come across anyone to beat Frank Tyson for a year or two in the 1950s. He made them shudder in Australia with his pace but, with the benefit of hindsight, he was never likely to last long because speed was his only weapon. His length and line varied by the delivery, so I suppose he was never destined to be anything other than a short-lived success. My old mate Alan Davidson was never the quickest, but with that left-arm action of his he could swing the ball both ways and it is not sentiment which prompts me to declare him one of the best of his kind.

I realise it is invidious to make comparisons, but what I am going to say now may come as a shock to a few people who look back on the 1930s as the heyday of cricket, particularly if they are England supporters who remember the "Bodyline Series" of 1932-3 with concealed affection. I have no hesitation in saying that if Harold Larwood, the great Nottinghamshire and England player, was performing today he would be branded as a "thrower". I have seen film of the "Bodyline Series" over and over again and, as a Test umpire, I am firmly convinced that he threw his quicker ball. As a professional umpire I would have certainly called him for an illegal delivery had he been around in my era. I don't say he did it every ball; just when he was striving for that little bit of extra pace. What is more, I am sure I would not have been alone in my condemnation. Other, more learned, judges have formed exactly the same opinion about Larwood, and it is a source of some wonderment to me that he was never under greater scrutiny during his finest, most infamous hour.

Harold Rhodes, the Derbyshire bowler who had a few matches for England, was branded a thrower and he was never able to escape the stigma. I played against him many times when I was at Somerset and I never thought he threw the ball. Having been labelled as such, his career was blighted for ever more and I often felt this to be unfair. Charlie Griffiths, the West Indian fast bowler, was another who never really recovered from being called for throwing. I toured Pakistan with Charlie in an international team and I am convinced he threw his quicker one, like Larwood but not like Rhodes. If anyone is suspect then I believe that for all concerned a quick verdict about the legitimacy of their action is needed. They should be filmed immediately and then either cleared once and for all, or condemned.

Sylvester Clarke had been under a cloud because there was

some doubt about the authenticity of his delivery, and it was unfair to him that the matter was allowed to ride without any clear guideline. He either threw or he didn't, and if it is considered that he did, then he should have been thrown out of the game for good – and that goes for all so-called chuckers.

Sometimes the word used to get around the county circuit that various players were a bit suspect, and such rumours had a nasty habit of spreading like a bush-fire. Perhaps it is right that as a retired umpire I should say here and now that there is no one in county or international cricket I consider to be a thrower. Talking of throwing, it calls to mind the sad case of Eric Bryant, a former colleague of mine at Somerset. He bragged openly before a match that he would throw, just to prove he could get away with it. He told his bewildered teammates that no umpire would spot him. He was wrong. He was spotted by Hugo Yarnold at Bath in 1960 and called for throwing. He never bowled again.

When it comes to spin bowlers, I consider Tony Lock and Jim Laker the best of the lot, as a pair. It is a saying in cricket that fast bowlers hunt in pairs, but I have found the top spinners have always done the same. Ramadhin and Valentine were a classic example in the 1950's, and in county cricket, Edmonds and Emburey built a reputation as a formidable force together, and as individuals. I suppose if I had to choose one supreme spin bowler, it would have to be Laker. I never knew how to cope with him as a player. He had everything; line, length, flight and variation. Towards the end of his career he left Surrey for Essex and I reckon I should have been out ten times in one innings as I vainly attempted to lap him, but it was a green wicket and I got away with it. It was at Surrey, though, in tandem with Lock, that he became a great bowler, and we at Somerset always dreaded taking them on when the wicket showed even the slightest inclination to turn. He could remove just about anybody, but I remember giving him some help once, and paying the penalty with my wicket.

We were playing Surrey at Weston-Super-Mare, where Laker was bowling around the wicket and the ball was turning square. It was one hell of a job just surviving. I noticed Surrey's skipper Peter May had Peter Loader fielding at fine leg. For a reason I shall never know, I called out to May that as far as I was concerned Loader was standing in the wrong position. May must have wondered what I was up to. He was even more stunned when I told him to move Loader around to square leg. Sure enough, he did. About an over or two later I lifted Laker about four or five feet off the ground to Loader at square leg where he clutched the catch to his chest. I had plotted my own downfall and then fallen gently into a trap completely of my own making. I will never know what possessed me to do all that.

Nor will I ever forgive myself for committing cricketing suicide when we played Nottinghamshire in the Gillette Cup. Andy Corran was bowling to me and I hit a return shot to him firmly along the ground. Corran fielded it and I was three feet out of my ground. He hesitated and I shouted, "Go on, throw the bloody thing." He did. It knocked out my middle stump and I was a goner for a duck. Afterwards he told me he would never have hurled the ball at my wicket had I not told him to.

Tony Lock relied on the quicker ball to get his wickets but flight was his big weapon. I suppose Ray Illingworth and Freddie Titmus in England will be considered better all-round players than Laker and Lock because they could bat a bit. Titmus was the last before Hadlee to do the 1,000 runs and 100 wickets "double" in an English domestic season, and it used to be said he was deaf in one ear, but I have to say that for a deaf man he had an incredible ability to hear the faintest of nicks from a bat.

When talking about the best bowlers it has to be said that nowadays there are fewer genuine tail-enders in professional cricket. The better teams tend to bat all the way down the order, which was always the case. Many spinners picked up cheap wickets at the end of an innings when the last couple of batsmen came in for a slog. Such a sight is rare now. That is why Bill O'Reilly was such an outstanding bowler. He could beat anyone with such a massive variety of wrong 'uns, leg spinners and one or two of his own patent.

George Tribe was the best of the left arm spinners of a conventional sort, but no review of spin bowlers would be complete without a few words about Derek Underwood. He was a difficult man to umpire because his foot had a tendency to stray over the front line. "Get your foot back," I would tell him two or three times an over, but he still no-balled more than he ought. That said, he was a magnificent bowler, particularly on a wet wicket. No one got runs against him at any level for very long. He was unique. I never saw anyone similar and I think I should pay tribute here to Alan Knott. Underwood was never an easy man to keep to but he made it look easy.

13
South Africa, the great all-rounders and the West Indies

WHEN SOUTH AFRICA were re-admitted to international cricket, it gave the game a massive boost. I have been to South Africa and, much as I enjoyed my visits, was never able to condone apartheid. Any system which discriminates on the basis of the colour of a man's skin deserves the contempt and scorn of the rest of the world.

What I dislike almost as much is the way politics have been allowed to intrude into sport, though I accept that this is now inevitable and is simply a fact of life. There is no way South Africa would have returned to major cricket while the apartheid regime survived, and, from a purely cricketing standpoint, I viewed this as a shame. We shall never know how great were Barry Richards, Mike Procter or even Graeme Pollock. They were all players with outstanding talent but, because they were never in a position to be subjected consistently to the pressures of Test cricket, we will never discover if they had the big-match temperaments to equal their undoubted skills.

The same has to be said about Clive Rice, Ken McEwan and Garth Le Roux. It is one thing to score runs and take wickets in county and provincial cricket; it is another to achieve the same level of performance against the world's best bowlers and batsmen in front of big crowds and television. I have seen many talented players who have never got the best out of their ability because of flaws in their character rather than defects in their technique. Sometimes it is the players with lesser ability who thrive in difficult, testing circumstances because they have that vital ingredient – a solid temperament.

South Africa, the great all-rounders and the West Indies

Like everyone who saw him at close quarter, I marvelled at the magnificent batting of Barry Richards and I have no real doubts that in his prime he would have adjusted to Test cricket around the world with consummate ease. Procter was such a wonderful competitor that he, too, would have had no trouble. So who lost out, apart form the players themselves, by their absence? The answer, in my opinion, is the cricketing public, starved as they are of big names and variety. I would go so far as to say Ian Botham saved the game in the 1980's. The South Africans would have added a whole new dimension to the international game and Procter might have been able to match Botham's prodigious deeds. A new Botham today would be a millionaire before he was 30. The public around the world is crying out for a great new talent and he could easily come from South Africa.

The average cricket fan wishes to see the best available and, while I agree it was unlikely ever to happen, I feel the West Indians, Pakistanis, Indians and Sri Lankan supporters would have loved to have seen those magnificent South African players in their prime. Some South Africans got into Test cricket through the back door of ancestral qualification or, in the case of Kepler Wessels, by emigrating. The Kerry Packer affair knocked the stuffing out of the international game. When the South Africans were allowed back, the whole game – and I don't mean just the white countries – received a real shot in the arm.

We certainly saw the best of the Pollock brothers, Peter and Graeme, and that extraordinary fielder Colin Bland before South Africa was banished from the scene. Bland established himself as the first of the professional cover fielders, whose ability to stop a ball, save runs and run out a batsman was almost above and beyond his ability as a middle order batsman. Since he showed how to hit a single stump from impossible angles, youngsters everywhere have been anxious to emulate him. He is the man I see as responsible for the death-or-glory boys who fling themselves around the field in pursuit of the ball as if their whole lives depended on it. Bland has a lot to answer for.

Standing the Test of Time

There is a common belief that since he appeared from Rhodesia, as it was then, to show how to field the ball, fielding everywhere has taken on a different dimension in the last 30 years. Here I must disagree. Bland's slipping and sliding have altered the way a ball is fielded but not, I hasten to add, necessarily improved it. I admit there are fewer poor fielders who need to be hidden discreetly from the action by their captains, but I contend that in the specialist positions like cover and slips, there are players no better than they ever were. My argument is that in the old days we fielded better technically with our hands. That may seem a curious statement, but let me explain. The great fielders of any generation have been able to do so with one hand. Not many can do so today. What is more, those same great fielders, Hammond, Cowdrey, Barry Richards and Greg Chappell to name but a few, have never needed to throw themselves around like some demented soccer goalkeeper. I used to tell many young cricketers that they would never run anyone out on their backsides. They would come off the field at the end of the day covered in green marks where they had collided violently with the turf time and again. I had no sympathy for their histrionic efforts. I am afraid I would pour scorn on those green marks. In my view they merely displayed a lack of ability.

I will concede, of course, that there have been some exceptional fielders, like Derek Randall and David Gower in England, but they serve only to exaggerate the technical mediocrity of so many others. It was as much as most of them could do to stop the ball, and I came to call them "Billy Goat fieldsmen" because they were always grovelling around on the ground and coming up covered in dirt and green marks, like a goat in a field. John Wright, the former Derbyshire and New Zealand opening batsman, was unquestionably the worst culprit. I admired John as a batsman and his easy-going nature made him one of the most popular players on the county scene. When it came to fielding it was a different matter. We used to share a joke about it, and the laugh was always on him. Before his team went out to field I would say to him: "I'll give £50 to the nearest hospital if you come off at the next interval without a green mark on you". No hospital ever benefited from my most generous offer.

Yet, while the fielding standards are deceptively poorer these days, in my estimation the calibre of wicket-keeper is comparatively high. Rod Marsh retired earlier than he might have done because he always struck me as being some way ahead of any other keeper in Australia. I suppose it is fair to say he looked a little untidy, rather like Gil Langley, but his appearance masked not only his great skill, but might even have detracted from his value as a team man to the Australian cause. Wally Grout and Don Tallon were cleaner wicketkeepers than Marsh, but at he end of the day the record book tells the proper tale and Marsh is streets ahead of his predecessors. Marsh was so far in front of his rivals in Australia that there was never any contest for his place when he was available.

In England there was always the debate about the virtues of Alan Knott and Bob Taylor. Knott's greater ability with the bat nudged him in front and, in fairness to him, I hardly ever saw him make a mistake behind the stumps. For all that, I would rate Taylor marginally the better keeper. He had the best pair of hands I have ever seen. I am positive that if England's county cricketers had been interviewed and polled on whom they preferred, Taylor would have won comfortably. However, it is not wicket-keepers who bring spectators through the turnstiles, and that after all is the number one consideration of all connected with the professional game. In my opinion it is the all-rounders who must bear much of the responsibility for keeping the turnstiles clicking. The game is desperate for a new Sobers or an new Keith Miller. Crowds everywhere will always flock to watch a Botham.

I suspect Clive Rice might have become an all-rounder of genuine international calibre had South Africa been playing Test cricket. But I don't share the view that Kapil Dev, Richard Hadlee, or even Malcolm Marshall, were Test-class batsmen and bowlers combined. Hadlee and Kapil Dev scored Test centuries and Marshall has come close to getting one, but in the case of Hadlee and Dev, these guys were essentially middle-order hitters. I cannot rank them as serious batsmen, capable of scoring runs on any type of wicket or in any circumstances.

Imran Khan had a great physique for a cricketer and the pin-up looks of a film star but don't let his mild-mannered attitude fool anyone. He took his cricket very seriously and, like all successful men, would compete as tenaciously on a Sunday afternoon as he did in a Test match. It is a great pity that injury hampered his progress over the years because he would surely have graduated among the all-time greats in the fullness of time had he been able to stay fit. Imran built a fearsome reputation when he moved from Worcestershire to Sussex to continue his county cricket. On the hard, heavily-grassed wicket at Hove he positively scared batsmen as he charged down the slope unleashing a series of sharply-rising deliveries. I was always a little glad it was not me having to face him because the discomfort of those who did was glaringly obvious at close quarters. Yet, at the same time, he could score runs with that regal ease of his which marked him out as a batsman of such a magnificence. But he could get very worked up. Don Oslear and I were obliged to report him for bad language when Sussex were playing Warwickshire at Edgbaston in 1983 as he attempted to find his feet again after a lengthy absence through injury. Willie Hogg, who bowled on the quick side of medium pace, got a ball to rise and smack him on the chest. The blow injured not only his body, but also hurt his pride. Referring to Hogg's own, more tail-end quality batting, Imran screamed down the wicket at him: "You never get close enough for me to hit you." It was a nasty moment and a little surprising to hear it coming from the man the Sussex supporters liked to call "The Prince". Oslear and I warned him such a statement was bringing the game into disrepute and he was subsequently severely reprimanded for his outburst.

Imran was still fired-up by this clash and, in the same match, was involved in another remarkable incident, and once more the unfortunate Hogg was again at the centre of it. Imran took two wickets in two balls and since Hogg, who as I say was not the world's best batsman, was next in, Imran fancied his chances of celebrating his return with a hat-trick. As we waited for Hogg to make his way to the crease from the pavilion, Imran turned to me and said: "I bet you £20 I get him for the hat-trick". It is not often an umpire gets such an offer and I was a little taken aback by it. Checking that it was indeed Hogg making his way out, I gave the matter due consideration before coming back to my senses. I was the umpire and I had no business to get involved in any wager. "If I was not standing here, I would take you on," I told him. Money may not have been about to change hands but my evident disbelief was enough to stir up Imran still further. He thundered in and you could all but hear Hogg's knees knocking together. I could hardly believe my eyes when a split second later, Imran's teammates were racing towards him to salute his hat-trick. It was some minutes before I could offer my humble congratulations. I will never underestimate the man again, but I often think what might have happened had £20 been riding on it. I could be very obstinate over lbw shouts. Imran took six for six in 4.3 overs that day.

As for Botham, cricket owes him a huge debt of gratitude. I find it difficult to comprehend the number of people who continually sniped at him. I suppose it is the old problem of building someone up into a superman and then knocking him down. I felt desperately sorry for him. Botham single-handedly prevented the game drifting into decline, and I am amazed that those people who so applauded his exploits against Australia in 1981, and in many other matches before and since then, turned on him and reviled him for being over-weight, lazy, rude and unfit. You have to understand the man. I love him, and I don't say that because we are both Somerset men. He played his cricket like I did – to win. His problem was that because he had such a sensational career in all respects, he was a victim of his own success. He was expected to score a century or take five wickets every time he took the field anywhere in the world and the pressure to do that must have been intolerable.

Standing the Test of Time

I believe it is good that he has such great common-sense and has been able to put it all in perspective. A lesser man would have crumbled under the intense way in which he was scrutinised. How he has survived I shall never know. He went the best part of ten years without a proper rest, but at least he was shrewd enough to know when he needed to take life a little easier. I know some critics in Somerset thought he was using them, but I consider this most unfair. I have seen him in action on their behalf on many an occasion and I can tell them he never gave less than his best. He wanted a wicket every ball, and yet he alone refused to believe this was simply not possible. At the end of a day, he will say to me in the bar: "Give the big fella a large gin and tonic." To my bosom pal I say: "Cheers, the game needs you". I only wish his critics shared my sentiments.

Mike Procter would surely have been one of cricket's outstanding names had he been able to perform at the highest level. He had the talent; he had the temperament. The stages provided by Gloucestershire, Natal, Western Province and Rhodesia, however, were too small for a man of his genuine all-round proficiency. Not that Procter ever felt sorry for himself, or took umbrage over the fact that he had been denied a proper setting for his talents because of a political situation over which he had no control. On the contrary. For Gloucestershire he gave 100 per cent, and he guided his adopted county to two cup final wins with inspirational performances along the way. In his combative attitude he was similar to Botham and not unlike an Aussie in character – tough, competitive and determined to win however small or trivial the prize.

I had the greatest admiration for him, but he could be a bit of a handful to an umpire. I recall having to tell him to cut down on the short-pitched deliveries when I thought he was overdoing them. He took it badly, but it was always necessary with Procter to show him who was boss on the field. No disrespect to the Gloucestershire boys but Procter virtually carried them for a decade, batting at number four or five, opening the bowling and then resorting to spin later in the innings. At Cheltenham, at that most picturesque of grounds, Procter had a rare duel with Keith Boyce, the West

South Africa, the great all-rounders and the West Indies

Indian all-rounder who played for Essex at the height of his career as a big-hitting middle order batsman and new ball bowler. Boyce was a fine, highly capable cricketer playing that day for the West Indies in 1973. When he was batting, Procter subjected him to a barrage of bouncers, partly from the belief that Boyce liked to hook and partly because I think there may have been a little needle between the two. Boyce did exceptionally well to survive and he only did so with a certain amount of luck. When Gloucestershire batted Procter discovered he had to face his first ball from Boyce, who could obviously see the chance for a spot of revenge. Boyce's first ball was the quickest I ever saw him send down, and it was a bouncer every bit as vicious as anything Procter had been mustering earlier. Procter ought to have been expecting it, but he wasn't. The ball nearly pole-axed him as he collapsed in an undignified heap with his cap about six feet away from his head behind the stumps. Procter was clearly shaken as Boyce scowled at him from the other end of the wicket. There was no love lost. "The biter bit," said a very satisfied Boyce as he went past me back towards his mark. Revenge had been sweet. That aside, it was not often that we ever saw Procter have the worst of a tussle. He was a magnificent player and a credit to his country.

For my money though, Keith Miller and Sobers are in a class of their own as all-rounders. They had so much ability in every department of the game that it was almost unfair on the rest of us mere mortals. I rate them the best players of all time. I played against both players and it was remarkable how similar they were as individuals. Both loved a bet, a drink and a woman. Sometimes I thought Sobers lived the horses more than he did his cricket, and much the same could be said for Miller. They were both easy-going men totally at ease with their own prodigious talent and never arrogant or conceited. Miller and Sobers were good company, loved the companionship of other cricketers and enjoyed life to the full. Both had the incredible capacity to spend a night on the tiles and return next day fresh enough to win a match, literally off their own bats. They would each chat away during a match revelling in their own genius and good fortune. Neither worried about facts and figures - at least not of the cricketing type - and there was never any question of a darkened room for contemplation if they were ever out before they should have been. They had a wonderful free attitude to the game and I only wish a new Miller or a new Sobers was on the horizon. Like Botham, we need them.

When it comes to batsmen I have never seen anyone to touch Viv Richards. He is the best by a fair distance and that may surprise those who believe Bradman is the greatest there has ever been, but the game has changed. Bradman was a run-machine; a unique phenomenon. Richards was an instinctive genius. He saw the ball so much quicker than anyone I have ever come across and his technique, while not exactly textbook, was flawless. From a purist's point of view he probably played across the line too often, but he could get away with it. Viv's greatest shot was the one he played through mid-wicket off the middle stump. It was awe-inspiring to watch; one of the great shots of all-time and no less exciting for seeing it over and over again. Bradman could also hit the ball from any angle, and people like May and Cowdrey were very correct players, but what singled out Richards was his ability to go for his sixes. Now, I can hear many people saying that he capacity for six-hitting does not make for outstanding batsmanship, necessarily. I agree you don't have to hit sixes to be a top-class batsman, but Viv could hit any bowler out of the firing line at any time – and that is something none of the great names of the past have ever been able to do, not even Bradman. In the right mood, no one could bowl to him; he could be utterly destructive, and the same could never be said for Bradman. He preferred to accumulate his runs, not by murdering the bowling as Richards did.

That shot of Richards through midwicket has become a sort of trademark like another played by Roy Marshall, the West Indian opening batsman who played for the best part of two decades for Hampshire. Roy was a stunning talent and yet only played in four Test matches. I was a specialist gully fielder for Somerset and the first time we played Hampshire he slashed the ball over me off the top edge of his bat at a tremendous speed. I was not impressed. I put it down to a fair slice of luck and told him so. "Try that again, mate," I said in a feeble attempt to wind him up. Minutes later, with a flick of the wrist, the ball soared over my head for six as easy as they come. Roy looked at me and smiled. It must be one of the hardest shots to play, and you will never see it in any coaching manual, but there was not a hint of fortune about it. Somehow he had been able to develop this shot over gully which I had never seen before. It required a great eye for the ball, wrists of whiplash steel and a firm conviction in its success. Yet he did it again, year after year with unfailing accuracy. Some teams had a deep gully for him, but it brought him a massive number of runs, more a slash than a cut, and I only wish he had been playing in the age of the television because we may never see the like again.

Some batsmen, though, could never improvise or patent a shot in the manner of Richards and Roy Marshall. Most stuck firmly to what they had been taught at school and were never able to shake off the rule book. Frank Worrell, great though he was as a batsman, once admitted to being too correct for his own good. Worrell was a prince among conventional stroke-makers, but I remember when we were playing in the same Commonwealth team in India in 1949-50 when he literally could not get himself out. We were at the crease together in the Braybourne Stadium in Bombay and Worrell had stroked his way to an impeccable century, to the delight of the traditionally huge crowd. But he did not look as immaculate as his hundred had been. He called me for a mid-pitch chat. He was covered in sweat in the great heat and looking distinctly unhappy. He said: "I can't get out. I have been trying to get myself dismissed for ages. What shall I do?" I was surprised. It is not often you hear such an unorthodox plea for help. I told him to give a catch and head for a cooling drink in the pavilion. When he had made 109, Worrell was still there and had not so much as given the hint of a catch. He called me for another conference. "Bill," he said, "I do not know how to get out. I was taught never to give my wicket away. It is not in my nature to play a rash shot." I told him there was only one thing for it. To kick over his own stumps. Minutes later, and visibly distressed, he committed suicide by treading on his wicket. Never have I seen a man so guilty and yet so relieved as he made his way back to the shade to the tumultuous cheering of the masses, unaware as they were of what a curious dilemma had been confronting him.

For sheer discipline and dedication of spirit there has been no one to rank with Geoff Boycott. I have a great respect for Geoff. Like many outside Yorkshire I found him difficult to understand at times because he would very often end up in a muddle of his own making, particularly while he was batting. I could observe him getting more and more reluctant to play his shots during an innings, no matter how good or bad the bowling. Who knows what went through his mind while he was at the crease. I believe he could have been a far freer batsman than he allowed himself to be. Technically it was all there, but he will always be a mystery to friend and foe alike for his reluctance to let his undoubted quality have full rein. He left the game with a big balance, but was he able to say he had enjoyed himself? I have my doubts.

I suspect also that his beloved Yorkshire really ought to have done better during his tenure of 20 years or more. I had some fine verbal battles with Geoff over the years. He was not above a bit of umpire-baiting, though he never once showed any dissent at any of my decisions. For instance, he would get down to the bowler's end where I was standing and look down the track, muttering to himself. Then he would look at me and shake his head. "He's got to do a lot to get an lbw, Bill," he would tell me. I wasn't going to be intimidated, even by someone with his record. I would tell him equally adamantly that I made my decisions from where the bowler's arm finished and I would give lbw if I thought he was out. At least we knew where we stood.

At his best, Geoff was among the best players of my time. He certainly cannot be compared with Viv Richards, and the only player even close to him was his compatriot, Gordon Greenidge. In my estimation, Greenidge was playing in a sort of mental shadow of

Richards, and I sometimes feared he would never get the full recognition his mighty talent merited. Gordon is an introverted sort of character and this may have held him back a little because he was every bit as good as Richards when he got into his stride. Richards was lucky to have players like Greenidge and Desmond Haynes to see the shine off the new ball. No one, not even Richards, hits the ball as hard as Greenidge and he can defend as well.

Clive Lloyd has been a tremendous representative for the Caribbean countries over the years, but as a batsman I would not rank him among the greats of my lifetime. One of the best one-handed fielders I ever saw, he was somewhat fortunate to bat at six for the West Indies, but in fairness to him he has certainly made use of this prime position. He was one of the most receptive of captains and liked and admired by all who knew him.

14
Back to the Beginning

WHEN TIME ALONE plunges you into the unknown territory of retirement it is easy to look back on what might have been. I suppose I shall always regret not representing my country in a Test match. It is not something which niggles me every day now that, for the first time in my life, I have time on my hands. In any other era I might have earned myself a tour and even a cap, but I was competing against exceptional players for a place in the national team and I am left to content myself with the knowledge that I was genuinely unlucky.

I am the first to agree that I was not blessed with outstanding talent. I had a great eye for a ball, I was very competitive and I was prepared to work hard. But nature did not endow me with that little bit extra, and no amount of hard work could fully compensate for the absence of the flair which marks out the brilliant from the ordinary. When I see the very average talent of some of the players who have since worn the famous green and gold my heart sinks. I was born in the wrong era. These days there are plenty of Test and international matches, and had I been that crucial twenty years younger then I might well have fulfilled my dream.

I was, of course, a late starter, so that in my case it was not necessarily a case of ambition thwarted. I had never seen myself as a Test-class player and, although I never had any sense of inferiority, I was happy just to be playing for New South Wales and actually being paid to do so. In many respects I have had the last laugh. I may not have been part of Bradman's all-conquering 1948 tour party to England, but I at least can now look back on nearly 40 years of involvement in the game we all loved. Not many of Bradman's team can say that. I came into everything late. I was always at the veteran stage at the start of every facet of my career.

This merely made me more determined to be successful. I admit that Australians might look upon me as a sort of mercenary, shifting around the cricketing world for the highest rewards. I am equally sure they will not blame me. Had Colne not lured me to England in the first place, I would have been quite happy ultimately to have returned to some labouring job in and around Sydney and been perfectly happy with my memories of my brief flirtation with the big-time. I realise I came to England at a low personal ebb, but I have never regretted my move. I love England now every bit as much as I love my home country. People are much the same the world over and, while there have been times when I have not been able to understand the game's establishment in England, I have found them, deep down, to be as warm and friendly as any Australian. I am aware, every day of my life, that I am an Australian in exile - but there is no sense of alienation. This is my home now and it will be until I draw my last breath.

Everyone has twists and turns in their lives, pushing them along paths they had not anticipated. If Somerset had not persisted with their offer, I am sure I would today have been living in Blackpool. And if Somerset had not booted me out, prematurely in my estimation, I might not have been so keen to go on the list of first-class umpires. I enjoyed my time as an umpire as much as I had ever enjoyed playing, which may sound like an odd admission to those who believe there is no substitute for actually being involved as a player. I can see their point of view. In my heyday as a cricketer, I looked on the umpire as a sort of necessary evil, but after 16 years on the list, and with ten Tests under my belt, I came to realise what a skilled craft it was.

I will treasure my appearances in the Test arena as an umpire. I only wish they had been a little less controversial because, contrary to popular opinion, I have never sought the limelight. Test matches provided an extra dimension and the pressures were not easily overcome. I only hope that younger umpires will be able to cope with the demands being made on them at the highest level. It is a very different game now from the one I first came into as an official way back in 1969. It is harder, fiercer and downright nastier. I am not saying the pressures are beyond the control of any new men coming into the game. I am only issuing a warning. Players will push the rules to the limit without actually breaking them. There is no give and take. The old concepts of sportsmanship have long since gone. With that in mind, a young umpire can know what to expect. Players aren't going to make any allowances and there is no question of any help. I find this a sad state of affairs but I am not going to bleat about it.

Nevertheless, during my 16 years there was a noticeable cooling of attitudes; a scowl replaced a smile on the face of cricket and I hope there is soon a reversal to the days when the game was there to be enjoyed, even by professionals. I could understand this icy shift if standards were correspondingly better. But they are not. It is not as good a game as it used to be and it is played, if not in a spirit of hostility, then certainly with increasing desperation, at Test level particularly. The responsibility now lies with the legislators and the game's executive to keep a firm grip and I do not envy their task. To that end, I am pleased that so many people at the highest level, at Lord's and elsewhere, have the game at heart and will not easily relinquish their command. I deplore the advent of players' committees to sit in judgement on their teammates, as they do in Australia. This can only erode the power of the boards of control. Some players are beginning to think they are bigger than the sport itself, and it will be very dangerous if these men are not stopped. It is a wonderful game and it is up to all of us to make sure it is still a worthy example for impressionable youngsters.

From that fateful moment in 1948 when I packed all my belongings into a couple of trunks and said goodbye to my homeland, I have only returned to Australia twice. I first went back in September 1951 for six months to pick up my son, Ken. By that time my life was beginning to take shape in England and, after the traumas and unhappiness of the period just before I left Australia, I wasn't keen to return on a permanent basis. I had married Betty and I was enjoying life in the industrial north of England. I know

Betty loves Australia, but we never considered going back for good. I had a good contract with Colne and if I had been seduced into going home, it would have been to a job outside cricket.

It was something like 24 years before I next set foot on home soil, and even then I only went back because someone else was paying for it. Out of the blue, I got a call from the organisers of Australia's "This Is Your Life". They wanted me to go to Sydney to appear as a guest in a programme they were doing on Jack Neary, who apparently, in my absence, had been a key figure in the building of the now world-famous Sydney Opera House. Jack had been a school-mate in Brooklyn and we had long since lost touch. I don't suppose I had seen him for 30 years and I was amazed that they had even been able to link me with him. Jack had obviously done well for himself and I had no hesitation in agreeing to fly home, all expenses paid for Betty and myself.

It is curious how that little school in Brooklyn, with its very rudimentary facilities, had managed to produce several people who went on to make their mark on the outside world. Vic Patrick, now a publican in Sydney, was another contemporary of mine who made his name as a boxer. Vic and I started as boxers together, but whereas I took some terrible hidings during my 28 straight wins, Vic soon moved up into a higher class altogether. I fought because I enjoyed it, because I was reasonably good at it and because I made a few pounds out of it. Vic was a lightweight who had class; far more than his stable-mate and school-friend. To the excitement of an entire nation, Vic was given the chance to fight for the world title at Rushcutters Bay in Sydney against Todd Morgan. The whole city came to a standstill and Vic was undisputedly in the lead on points until the 14th round when the referee stopped the fight, unconvinced Vic was fit to continue.

Then there was my best friend, Ian Cross, who worked with me on every job I had after leaving school. Ian took up cycling in a big way and before long became the world quarter-mile sprint champion, which he achieved at Lidcombe Oval, the cricketing home of the Benaud family. I must remember George Cook. He

165

went on to become a sailing title-holder in Australia and achieved an international reputation. Even so, it was Neary who carved the most permanent niche for himself in Australian history, and it was a pleasure to be asked to honour him.

I had ten days to get ready for the long journey to Sydney and I had little time to wonder what would be waiting for me. When I got there, I could hardly comprehend the changes of three decades. Sydney was a new and cosmopolitan city, the forest of skyscrapers an astonishing contrast to the rows of squat little houses with their uniform red roofs that I remembered from my youth. As we were driven in from the airport in the south, I gazed in awe at what greeted me. I could have been on the moon for all I recognised. Every now and then on the journey to our hotel on the north shore I would see a brief glimpse of something familiar - and then it was gone again, hidden from view by a massive building which had sprouted in my 30 years away. The whole experience was very unnerving and I felt ill at ease as we attempted to settle in. I had been looking forward to rediscovering old haunts and old faces, naively imagining that it would all be as I had left it. How wrong I was!

One of the first things I did was to buy a map to find out where I was. Little roads were now highways, old pubs were now shopping centres and famous landmarks were dwarfed by vast concrete towers. Sydney was now an international city and it was definitely not the place I had known so well in my youth. What struck me also was the number of Italians, Greeks, French and many other nationalities who had chosen to make their home there, and it was still a greater shock to hear them speak with an Australian accent. I had managed to retain mine in spite of my many years away, but inevitably I had picked up one or two peculiarly British phrases which all but marked me out as a foreigner. I had acquired the Lancashire habit of calling all women "love", and while I thought nothing of it, the utterance brought some startled responses from the female population of Sydney. They must have thought I was crackers!

It was one of the little marks left by the passing of time, but in the days leading up to the show it was a real struggle to come to terms with what they had done to my home-town. Betty suggested we hire a car to get a closer look at this vibrant new place. I refused point blank. There was no way I was going to get in a car and negotiate the road system. I was scared by the very prospect, and yet I thought nothing of driving in the centre of London and other big English cities. It was just that I knew London, Manchester, Birmingham and other places. I did not know my own city and I was quietly ashamed.

One of the worst aspects of waiting to take part in the programme was the ban on getting in touch with anyone I knew in case it somehow gave the game away. I had brothers and sisters living in Sydney and my father was also somewhere out there, but I was forbidden from making contact. I am not the world's best letter-writer and I had rather lost my way when it came to maintaining our family links. I had written often enough but we had grown apart. It was difficult to explain the sort of life I was now leading in England, hunting and shooting in the rolling Quantock Hills of Somerset, and just as Sydney was a different place from the one I knew, they too had been changed by circumstances and time itself.

The big day came and Jack was stunned to see me in traditional "This Is Your Life" style. I met many old friends and, although they had obviously aged, like all genuine friends we carried on as if we were still in the first flush of youth. It was a magnificent occasion. We were well looked after by the television company and the reunions took away some of the feeling of disorientation I had felt upon my return.

While I was in Sydney I took the opportunity to make a poignant journey down memory lane. I made my way to the Sydney Cricket ground for a spot of unashamed nostalgia. The ground was deserted but I could all but hear the roars and applause of the 40,000 crowds which, in those days, were part and parcel of state matches. I learnt with some displeasure that New South Wales feel they have done well if more than a couple of thousand now pass through the turnstiles. That is what television, too many one-day internationals and too many Tests has done. But on this particular day, it was a chance to look back. I wandered out to the wicket to survey the scene on my own. There might have been a couple of groundsmen busying away elsewhere in the stadium, but if they were, I did not notice them. I stood in the middle and thought of the big crowds I had played in front of here at the SCG; I thought also of what the game had done for me over the previous 28 years; I thought of the many places cricket had taken me to around the world in ten tours; of all the major stadia I had played in; of all the famous names I had played with and against. Cricket had been good to me and it was at this moment that I came to pay it a silent tribute. Multi-millionaires could not have bought the experiences the game had given me and, as I acknowledged my good fortune, a lump came into my throat. It was an emotional moment, one of the most distinct of my life, and as I wiped away a tear or two I must have been a strange sight. The ghosts of 28 years in this wonderful sport rattled through my mind and I looked skywards and quietly said my thanks.

I left Sydney soon afterwards and I have not been back since. It is an ambition of mine to make at least one more trip home and now that I have retired I dare say I shall get the chance. In some ways I would have liked to have been part of the Sydney success story, if only because most people retain some affection for their home town out of nostalgia as much as any other reason. The Sydney I saw in 1976 was not the Sydney I remembered as a young man but the loyalty will always remain.

Now, though, Somerset is my home and I am deeply fond of it, more even I think than many of those born and bred in the county who have never lived elsewhere. I love the place and I love the warm, West Country ways of the people. The countryside is beautiful and I never cease to marvel at the way it changes constantly and the way the seasons are in such sharp contrast to one another. I had my two acres outside Taunton where I kept some chickens and some sheep, stocking up my deep-freeze with my own produce and living off the land long before it became fashionable. I shoot rabbits

168

and, when I first came down from Lancashire, regularly enjoyed stag-hunting on those magnificent Quantock Hills which begin barely four or five miles from my bungalow.

There are people in the town of Taunton who have never even been up into the Quantocks. They will never know what they have been missing because for me they have become a source of recreation and, in a strange sort of way, an inspiration. The local people were quick to accept me and to take me to their hearts. I can never walk very far in the town without being stopped by someone. Or from the other side of the street somebody I have never seen would shout: "Morning, Bill." As I struggle to put a name to the face, I shout back: "Watch yer, mate," and wander on still trying to work out the identity. I love it, though. I reckon I am better known in Taunton than the mayor himself and I enjoy the recognition. It certainly makes shopping trips more interesting. I find it hard to imagine living anywhere other than Somerset now. It has become part of me and when I returned to the county after my umpiring had taken me to other parts of the country, I would salute the Somerset name-plate as I passed the county border. I suppose it must have looked a little strange for drivers going in the opposite direction to see a man on his own stiffly saluting a boundary marker, but this is what it means to me now. I shall continue to offer my salute to Somerset, the most wonderful place in the world.

I will never take either Somerset or what I have got from cricket for granted. I remember walking around the sights of London one day after a match had been rained off. I took in St. Paul's Cathedral and the Tate Gallery and marvelled, like a camera-clicking Japanese tourist, at the wonder of it all. Cricket has enabled me to see such places. Had I stayed in Sydney I would surely have missed out on the great treasures of the world. Indeed, if I had to offer any advice to a young cricketer it would be to never take anything for granted. For someone like me it was a struggle to make a living out of the game because the money just wasn't there. It is a different tale today. Sponsors are falling over themselves to put in the cash which means a good living for all. They should cherish and nurture their talent, never abuse it. They should work at their skills and take pride in their good fortune at being involved in a game they love.

`One of the side effects of making a late entry into professional cricket has been the realisation that, for many people, watching cricket is a relaxation and they will pay to see good play in the best possible atmosphere. The game might be better if a few of our youngsters came to terms with their privileged life and acted accordingly. Ironically, I have great faith in the young of today and in the strength of cricket. I believe it will survive and prosper as long as it remains in the right hands. Cricket has been good to me and it will be for others if they treat it with the same respect.

I have many friends around the world, a nice home and car and a bank balance which will prevent us from starving in our old age. When I retired I was touched by the many presents I received from people within the game, and what made them all the more humbling was the spirit in which they were offered. I almost got the impression some were sorry to see me go. Essex, as I told you, made their own presentation in their own unique way. Others were just as generous. The Glamorgan boys gave me a litre of scotch, Gloucestershire came up with a half gallon of sherry. Over the years they must have formed the impression I liked a drink or two. Yorkshire's cricketers spotted my weakness for gin, while Worcestershire kindly gave me a photograph. Hampshire signed a cricket stump on my behalf, and, most touchingly, the other umpires on the first-class list clubbed together to buy a silver tray inscribed to Betty and myself. The boys from Middlesex gave a club jumper embellished with the club crest and the beneficiary's tie. Somerset, of course, came up with a magnificent present, a set of glasses and a decanter. I am not often stuck for a sentence or two but it is difficult to say anything at the time which fully conveys my thanks. Sincerely, I shall miss them all.

My retirement was complete when my bosses, the Test and County Cricket Board, gave me a fantastic send-off with an inscribed cabinet case. I sometimes wonder what I had done to deserve such treatment considering all the little crises I had run into over the years. Indeed, I was particularly lucky to get such a fine and heart-felt present from Lord's bearing in mind the disaster of my first ever match as an umpire. Middlesex were playing Essex and the Middlesex lads could see I was nervous and anxious to make an impression with several important people watching my progress from the stands. The last thing I wanted to do was make a bad start. Unfortunately the jokers among the Middlesex team were intent on making sure everything went wrong!

The great wits in the Middlesex dressing-room in those days were Peter Parfitt, John Murray, Fred Titmus and John Price, and they had obviously hatched a plot to make my first morning an utter misery. After about two overs it had gone well and my nerves were just beginning to settle. Then suddenly I was in a hopeless mess. I was convinced the next over had run its six-ball course but, just as I was about to call "over", I noticed Parfitt, Murray, Titmus and the others in the slips and behind the wicket getting down to await the next ball. Price started to return to his mark to bowl. The words choked in my throat. I thought I had mis-counted the number of balls and decided the best thing to do was remain silent. Price duly bowled.

The next over was even worse. After what I thought were five deliveries the wicket-keeper and the slips started coming down to my end as if it was the end of the over. I was in a terrible mess. I had obviously mis-counted again. But, as I lifted the stones from my pocket to count the number of balls, Price grabbed his sweater, the balls spilled everywhere and, by the time I had tremblingly retrieved them and shouted "over", the players were all in position for the next over in any case. I had no idea what was going on. The Middlesex players started to snigger as they surveyed my shocked state at square leg. Minutes later, Parfitt came over and in mock condemnation and said: "What's up with you? First you allow a seven ball over and then you don't say anything when five are bowled. You'll never make it as an umpire."

I was in a daze and I was still gathering my wits at square leg some time later when a catch came my way. I reacted as a player, and not as an umpire would have done, and attempted to catch it. I was so embarrassed I could not eat my lunch. The other umpire, John Langridge, attempted to console me as I rang out the sweat from my singlet, which had become saturated in nervous perspiration. "It can only get better," he told me. It did, but a highly-amused Billy Griffiths, an important man then at Lord's, could not contain himself when he knew the joke was out. "Why didn't you catch it?" he inquired. I had no answer. I was convinced I was finished.

Luckily cricket in those days was played in a different spirit and the jape was explained to me later. They all laughed and I might have done as well, but I was too busy contemplating what I thought was the damage to my career! All was forgiven and the rest is the history you have just been reading. In the meantime I salute Somerset and I salute cricket. My innings is over but long may the game prosper.

15
Epilogue

MOST OF WHAT you've just been reading was written some 14 or 15 years ago, soon after I had retired from umpiring. I had hoped my bosses at Lord's would look kindly on what I had said - but they didn't. The manuscript was taken to Donald Carr, then the secretary of the TCCB, and he made it clear that he thought I had overstepped the mark with some of my comments. He did not approve, and since I was under contract for a couple of years after my retirement, and bound by the terms of that contract to say nothing of importance, I had to keep quiet, much to my annoyance. It has always struck me as absurd that even umpires needed approval for what they said, but that's the way it was.

Much as I love the game I'm glad I am not umpiring these days. I wince for my old colleagues when I see their every decision replayed to death on television and I know how they must be feeling. Some of my old mates tell me how undermined they feel by having their every decision analysed again and again. Everyone makes mistakes and the umpire has to make an instantaneous choice, for better or worse. Their job is made no easier these days by the lack of walkers. When I played and when I first started umpiring so many batsmen walked because they knew they were out and no decision needed to be made. These days the umpires get absolutely no help. I spend a lot of the season watching matches at the County Ground at Taunton and unless it's obvious he's out you won't see a batsman budge from his crease until the dreaded finger is raised, even if he knows he's out. The decision has to be made for him, which I find despicable in many respects. Fair enough, the umpire is there to make the decisions, but if a batsman knows he's nicked it he should bloody well go and not wait to be told. I hate the sight of batsmen making a slow way back to the pavilion, staring at their bats or shaking their heads in silent disbelief. That's dissent in my book and should be stamped out.

Appealing has also reached ludicrous proportions and that's another thing which annoys me greatly. Bowlers almost on all fours begging and pleading for the umpire to give the batsman out and huge, arms-aloft shouts bellowed from square leg for lbw. I suppose it's all part of the dressing room strategy, whatever that might be. Never give the umpire a moment's peace, and if he turns down two big appeals he might feel duty bound to uphold a third. I suspect many of the more traditional followers of the game will blame the Aussies for introducing such tactics, but every other nation has quickly followed them, bar none. I remember umpires were summoned to Lord's for a meeting about the increase in the volume and frequency of appealing and we were told to speak to the captains if we felt it was excessive. But, by the looks of things now, it's here to stay.

This is going to make me sound like an old grouch, but there's a couple of other things I find ridiculous about today's cricket. One is the incessant chat on the pitch and, in particular, where the fielding side applauds a bowler for hitting the middle of a batsman's blade. "Well bowled", they shout. And they say the same when the ball passes the off stump by about a foot and the batsman doesn't even need to play it. I can't imagine ever being told I had bowled well when I had hit the middle of the bat. If I had, I would have thought someone was taking the what's his name. All wicket-keepers do it and I know it drives umpires mad.

How strange it is now to think back on the niceties of cricket when I started. It all seems faintly old-fashioned and from another ordered and mannered world. All the players wore their club blazers at lunch and it used to be that the home captain would go into the opposition dressing room and invite his counterpart into the dining room for the meal. He also took him in a drink at the end of the day. I know life moves on, and I speak very much as an old player, but a little formality never did any harm. After all, cricket is still a very formal game and some would say the formality is part of its beauty.

As for helmets — red ones, blue ones, white ones, yellow ones — I find them at best odd and at worst plain bloody stupid. I'm not against them in principle, and they were introduced when the West Indies' fast men were being allowed to bowl bouncers all day long without anyone telling them to aim at the stumps occasionally. I can see why they came into the game, but in my view there is little need for them now, and the sight of them atop so-called class batsmen when they are facing medium-paced trundlers or, worse still, spinners, says little for their technique or their bravery. There are hardly any fast bowlers around now, or at least fast enough to worry good batsmen, and I can't understand why numbers one to eleven all feel obliged to wear one, even in limited overs matches. Viv Richards never wore one and would have taken it as an affront to his dignity if anyone had suggested he should. If batsmen had better technique there would be no need for helmets. I like to watch village cricket when I can and I'm amazed the number of village cricketers who wear helmets and arm guards as some sort of fashion accessory, even when they are facing bowlers who can't get the ball above stump-high.

As for television replays, they are a fact of life but I know many of my old pals fear their power is being taken away and their role as the game's only arbitrators is being diminished. One of them told me only recently how the confidence to make a decision has been eroded and they fear giving any kind of verdict while a television camera is present. Even for the most obvious run out umpires are waiting for the slow motion camera to do their job for them.

I'm glad umpires are making regular checks on the state of the ball during a match because I know only too well how tempting it is to tamper with the seam. In my playing day the seam was made of a thick twine and it was easily lifted, but the balls used these days have a nylon seam which is far harder to raise. Everyone did it, almost without exception, and when I became an umpire I knew what I was looking for. I remember pulling up one bowler for blatantly picking the seam and I said to him: "Don't do it." He looked at me in astonishment. "How can you tell me not to pick the seam when you were one of the best in the business at doing that in your playing career?" I almost took his comment as a compliment, but then I thought better of it. "Thanks for saying so, but I'm an umpire now and I'm telling you to stop what you are doing."

One day some brave umpire is going to get fed up also with those batsmen who use their pads as the first form of defence. I feel sorry for those spinners who are thwarted by pads thrust down the wicket by batsmen totally unable to read the delivery they are about to face. I would like to see umpires give these guys out once they've done it a couple of times, but I don't know what sort of support they would get from officialdom. Mostly it's done by inferior batsmen against good bowlers and I reckon they've got away with that tactic, if it is a tactic, for too long.

My concern is for the state of cricket. I still see plenty of it in my capacity as a sort of host and raconteur at Taunton, where Blundells School have a hospitality box. My job is to talk to guests, and talking has never been a problem for me, while myself and Betty are treated to the most marvellous four-course lunches in return. Blundells is near Tiverton in Devon and is still a cricketing school. Vic Marks, Hugh Morris and Jeremy Lloyds are all old boys. Ted Crowe, who is responsible for the organisation, spotted me through his binoculars one day sitting in the distance near the main gate and he kindly offered me the chance to become their resident greeter and speaker. Now from my position on high I can look down on the players of today and try to work out what is going wrong with the sport we all love.

I fear four-day cricket in England has not really worked. The public have shown no great appetite for it and I think they would prefer matches to be played over three days. Certainly among regular spectators I know that is the case. Lord MacLaurin feels duty bound to shake up the game, but for the life of me I can't see a two-tier county system working. Gates are poor enough now but there is no way two divisions will make the slightest difference to the size of attendances, and it's hard to imagine life in the second of the two divisions being much fun to play in or watch. Above all, it's not going to raise standards, and all the while the standard of player in county cricket remains so mediocre that nothing will change. This is what should be addressed.

Tampering with the county system is not going to make the slightest bit of difference while there are so few top class players for others to emulate and spectators to watch. In county cricket now I can't think of a home grown-player people would make an effort to see in action. Where have all the top class players gone? There are too many guys out there who are simply not good enough. They have huge technical deficiencies, bad attitudes and no desire to improve. They say they want to reduce the number of matches so that more time can be spent in the nets, but should that happen and, if they are honest, they know they will not use the extra time to work on their problems. Some people tell me that uncovered wickets should be reintroduced. At least that way batsmen and bowlers would learn to play in all conditions, but in my view it wouldn't make a jot of difference. Spectators and sponsors want to see cricket, and that's what they pay a lot of money to do. They don't want the sight of an empty playing field while the sun is shining and when the only action is provided by the groundstaff trying to get the pitch playable.

I suspect that cricket may not enjoy the place in people's hearts in this country as it once did. My grandchildren love their football, all of them Manchester United fans, but only young Lloyd, who's nine, has any interest in cricket. Yet spectators warmed to the spectacular fielding of Jonty Rhodes when the South Africans were in England in much the same way they had Colin Bland 30 or more years before. Both of them self-taught and almost amateurish in their delight in their own special talent. Yet we play cricket seven days a week in this country and have no one to compete with Rhodes. They tell me that fielding is much improved, but being able to dive doesn't make a great fielder. How often do you see the dying art of being able to field one-handed on the run? Not often, because they prefer to dive, attempting to field with their bodies and not their hands as they should have been taught. What are the coaches doing? Just about every county has felt obliged to hire expensive foreign coaches, but the overall standard of county cricket remains poor.

Yet the opportunities for talented youngsters to progress have never been better. At Taunton they have a fantastic indoor school with facilities to rival any in the world and there are queues of children waiting to use them. You get the impression they are only using the nets because there is nothing else to do or because parents are busy and need somewhere to dump them for an afternoon. Even young professionals don't work as hard at their game as they should. I noticed at Taunton recently how the Derbyshire lads were running around the pitch to warm up and it was always Kim Barnett, the oldest player in the team, who was in front.

Only a few years ago it was unthinkable that Yorkshire should import foreign players but now they wouldn't be without one, so it just seems that kids in England either don't like the game or are not prepared to work at it. They don't know what they are missing because for those of us bitten by the cricketing bug there is no game better. Will there ever be another Botham or another Hutton? From what I see there are none on the horizon, but all the while there are enthusiasts at all levels there is always hope. It only needs one lad to come through, as Tim Henman has in tennis, to rekindle interest in the whole sport.

As an Australian I find Shane Warne a wonderful talent and Muralitharan was a revelation when the Sri Lankans played in England, and I'm pleased his action has been cleared. If there is a benefit to be had from slow motion television replays it's that they show he does not throw, as many people suspect he did. For at least four years I opened the Somerset innings against Harold Rhodes and I never thought he threw but the great umpire Sid Buller was convinced he did and duly called him, although I'm not sure his opinion was shared by his fellow umpires of the time.

Talking of Buller, I reckon he and Arthur Fagg were models for any young umpires. They never rushed a decision, always taking their time before making their choice, and the reason I suspect is that they never felt threatened, either by bad marks from grudging captains or from getting the sack. Believe me the fear of being fired was always prevalent when I was an umpire and it's very much the case now. I suppose cricket was more fun even not so long ago and it should be fun now. I know this makes me out to be something of a curmudgeon, but it is only a game. We all felt, players and umpires, that we were lucky to be involved and be paid for what we did, and I wonder how many players now feel the same.

In my playing days Dai Davies, the old Glamorgan player, was a favourite of mine because in the nicest possible way I made sure his glass of Guinness was always filled when we were in the pub after play. "Thank you very much, Bill," he used to say as I ordered him another. Odd how many decisions went my way next day. Ron Lay was also a much respected umpire in my playing time because of his gentle smile and his amiable approach to his job. He appeared to enjoy himself and the players responded in the same manner. He once rejected a stumping appeal off my bowling because he could not see from his position at square leg the crease line where Frank Tyson had gouged out a huge hole with his run up when we played against Northamptonshire. It always surprised me that Ron never got a Test match because I'm sure he would have been a big success. In my umpiring time David Constant and Alan Whitehead were the men I considered to be the best, while Dickie Bird was, well, Dickie Bird. I blame Jim Laker, when he was a television commentator, for first making the public aware of Dickie's little on-field foibles and he quickly added a few more. At the end of a day's play Dickie liked his orange juice where others like me got stuck into the first pint of the evening, and while some umpires went off to a restaurant exploring new towns and cities, Dickie preferred his fish and chips in his hotel room while watching television.

At the start of each season each umpire got a list of where he was to go and with whom he would be standing. You always knew who among them would be ready for a good time and who among them would keep to themselves and save as much on expenses as they could. There were several with whom you didn't want to be sharing a week, I can tell you. Dave Halfyard, player of note in his time, had a reputation for being a bit of a loner, but one evening we went out together and he revealed a fantastic knowledge of good wines, and I found his company wonderful after that. The point is that players and umpires and officials all spent a lot of time talking about cricket at the end of a day's play in the pavilion bar, or in hotels and restaurants. There was a common desire to learn and to improve and I guess that may not be true now. I'm not suggesting players should get back home or to their hotel rooms at 2am, as we used to do, but there is no reason why a drink or two with the opposition at the end of a day's play should provoke frowns from well-paid overseas coaches.

Young players today tend to stick together and don't mix as much as we did and certainly none of the present Somerset players make any effort to pick my brains, welcome as they are. I have to say my relationship with Somerset might be better than it is though many of my pictures and artefacts are now in the county club's museum and I'm delighted about that. Apart from a time when Jack Birkenshaw was the county coach I have never been asked back to do any coaching there, but time moves on and I have had to accept the fact that at my age I never will. Even so, I am an honorary life member of Somerset, of which I am proud, but as an illustration of the gap between old and new I recall how when I was invited to cut the first sod to get work underway on the new pavilion neither Andy Caddick nor Mark Lathwell, who were performing the ceremonial task, said a word to me. All very odd, but typical of the generation gap.

All that's left for someone of 80 is to look back and I do so with great fondness. Betty and I have been married 50 years in September 1999 and we have a close-knit family living not far from our home in Taunton. Our eldest son Douglas is 44 and works in Bristol in a company specialising in air conditioning and electrical pumps. He is married to Carol and apart from Lloyd there is Katie, aged 12. Our other son is Timothy, who is 42, married to Lisa with children Thomas, aged 12, and ten year old James. He works for Securicor. Douglas played some club cricket but now sticks to golf and, unless Lloyd develops his interest in cricket, it's hard to see a new cricketing Alley on the horizon.

As for Betty, she used to play a bit of badminton and is a member of the women's institute. We are as devoted now to each other as we have ever been. Apart from cricket we drive out to the coast for a day occasionally, or up into the Quantock Hills, but we simply enjoy each other's company and there's always our garden where we spend a lot of time in the summer. Betty says my greatest asset as a person is my ability to communicate with anyone at a moment's notice. She says I'm placid and easy-going, and my biggest problem as far as she's concerned is my reluctance to have a decent row. As for her, I realise how lucky I have been. It wasn't love at first sight and we went out for nine months before we became a couple, because at the time I met her I had a girlfriend in Australia waiting for me, or so I thought. She's a brilliant mother, wife and cook and she's listened to me rabbiting on about cricket for half a century without complaint. Betty came from a family steeped in Lancashire league cricket, so it was not as big a pain for her as it might have been for some other wives. She also takes care of the financial side of our lives and always has done. She signs the cheques and deals with all the business. I like to think she has enjoyed her life in cricket as much as I have done mine. She has certainly never stopped me fulfilling what potential I had and from getting the best out of my sporting ability, such as it was.

From a technical point of view I would never have made it into the coaching manuals. I was driven by a fierce desire to make the best of myself, and with a good eye for a ball. Not much else apart from a raw and natural talent. I don't think purists liked my cross-bat style, but when I hit it the ball went a long way. I remember Arthur Gilligan saying once of me: "Where the hell does this fellow come from?" as I swished away in what he thought was an uncouth manner at the MCC bowling when I was playing for New South Wales. Denis Compton said to Walter Hammond when fielding at short leg to me in that match: "I think I will move back to Alley, if you don't mind." That's because I was trying to smack the ball around a bit, being no respecter of the opposition, no matter how well known.

Life is full of ifs. If I had been chosen for the 1948 tour of England I might have become an established Test star and never played professionally in England. But denied that opportunity I filled my boots in Lancashire earning colossal sums by the standards of post-war Britain. I was rich enough to eat steak several times a week, even when there was rationing, and to tip waiters an old £5 note. I know people who don't tip that amount now, let alone 1950. As I said, I never touched my basic wages and it was a wonderful time to be a professional cricketer in the leagues. If I had not come to England I would not have met Betty or settled here. True, I miss Australia, particularly the country areas where I grew up, but I have been more than compensated in other ways. If Blackpool had agreed to my request for a three-year contract I would have stayed there because we had bought a house in the town and loved it. I would have done some coaching and gone back to labouring and done none of the things for which I am best known.

I also think that if I had not been Australian, or at least someone not English, I might not have got on to the umpires' list when I packed up playing. It helped. The poacher turning gamekeeper. I can have no complaints about the way life has treated me. I still love my cricket and I watch every ball of every Test and limited overs international on television, enjoying those replays which were never available to me, thank goodness. Had I shown absolutely no ability or interest in cricket, where would I be?

My brothers and sisters did not stray very far from Brooklyn in their lives. They lived and died there, and I often wonder what they must have thought of me so far away from all we knew as children. I reckon at the very most I might have made my way to

Sydney, but if I'm honest I don't think I would have gone away from those Brooklyn oyster beds for long. Cricket opened up the world for me and gave me a very different life than the one I could have expected. If I have given some enjoyment along the way then I'm really very grateful.

W.E. Alley - First Class Career Statistics

TOTALS

Batting:

Matches	Inns	NO	Runs	HS	Ave.	100's	50's
400	682	67	19,612	221*	31.88	31	90

Bowling and fielding:

Runs	Wkts	Ave.	BB	5WI	10WM	Ct
17,421	768	22.68	8-65	30	1	293

Year-by-year analysis

BATTING:

Year	Country	Inns	NO	Runs	Hs	Ave
1945/46	Australia	8	1	485	129*	69.28
1946/47	Australia	3	1	56	43*	28.00
1947/48	Australia	5	0	56	36	11.20
1949/50	India	28	9	1,255	209*	66.05
1957	England	62	2	1,540	108	25.66
1958	England	58	2	1,318	89	23.53
1959	England	54	4	1,823	155	36.46
1960	England	42	7	807	110*	23.05
1961	England	64	11	3,017	221*	59.96
1962	England	58	6	1,915	155	36.82
	Rhodesia	4	0	128	55	32.00
1963	S. Africa	9	0	232	77	25.78
	England	38	2	1,076	105	29.88
	Pakistan	2	0	101	68	50.50
1964	England	47	3	1,332	140	30.27
1965	England	48	6	861	110	20.50
1966	England	51	3	1,104	115	23.00
1967	England	46	4	1,244	136	29.61
1968	England	49	4	1,219	110	27.08

BOWLING:

Year	Country	Overs	Mdns	Runs	Wkts	Ave
1946/47	Australia	7	0	42	0	-
1947/48	Australia	17	2	59	3	19.67
1949/50	India	61	20	138	0	-
1957	England	572.4	144	1,412	71	19.88
1958	England	519.1	111	1,256	56	22.42
1959	England	530.3	120	. 1,358	58	23.41
1960	England	731	206	1,679	73	23.00
1961	England	624.1	175	1,571	62	25.33
1962	England	947.1	256	2,323	112	20.74
1963	S. Africa	69	16	184	4	46.00
	England	401	148	758	39	19.43
	Pakistan	3	0	10	0	-
1964	England	650.4	213	1,365	64	21.32
1965	England	774	271	1,525	76	20.06
1966	England	519	170	1,015	50	20.30
1967	England	611.5	214	1,166	59	19.76
1968	England	523.5	184	1,229	36	34.13

Individual Performances

FIRST CLASS CENTURIES:

111	New South Wales	v South Australia	Adelaide	1945
119	New South Wales	v Australian Services	Sydney	1946
129*	New South Wales	v South Australia	Sydney	1946
168*	Commonwealth XI	v Indian Services	New Delhi	1949
209*	Commonwealth XI	v West Zone	Poona	1949
206*	Commonwealth XI	v C. C. of India	Bombay	1950
108	Somerset	v Worcestershire	Worcester	1957
155	Somerset	v Gloucestershire	Taunton	1959
103	Somerset	v Glamorgan	Weston	1959
110*	Somerset	v Sussex	Taunton	1960
211*	Somerset	v Warwickshire	Nuneaton	1961
183* & 134*	Somerset	v Surrey	Taunton	1961
156	Somerset	v Northamptonshire	Northampton	1961
155*	Somerset	v Yorkshire	Taunton	1961
150*	Somerset	v Surrey	The Oval	1961
134	Somerset	v Australia	Taunton	1961
123*	Somerset	v Nottinghamshire	Worksop	1961
120	Somerset	v Lancashire	Bath	1961
117	Somerset	v Essex	Weston	1961
102	A.E.R. Gilligan's XI	v Australia	Hastings	1961
155	Somerset	v Kent	Gravesend	1962
131*	Somerset	v Lancashire	Glastonbury	1962
102	Somerset	v Gloucestershire	Taunton	1962
105	Somerset	v Kent	Gillingham	1963
140	Somerset	v Derbyshire	Chesterfield	1964
110	Somerset	v Northamptonshire	Northampton	1965
115	Somerset	v Nottinghamshire	Nottingham	1966
110*	Somerset	v Glamorgan	Taunton	1966
136	Somerset	v Worcestershire	Glastonbury	1967
110	Somerset	v Kent	Weston	1968

TEN WICKETS OR MORE IN A FIRST CLASS MATCH

10-61 Somerset	v Hampshire	Bournemouth	1957

SIX WICKETS OR MORE IN A FIRST CLASS INNINGS

6-22	Somerset	v Hampshire	Bournemouth	1957
6-39	Somerset	v Leicester	Leicester	1958
8-65	Somerset	v Surrey	The Oval	1962
6-42	Somerset	v Leicestershire	Ashby de la Z	1962
6-48	Somerset	v Nottinghamshire	Nottingham	1962
6-116	Somerset	v Worcestershire	Bristol	1964
6-40	Somerset	v Hampshire	Bath	1965
7-58	Somerset	v Sussex	Weston	1966
6-63	Somerset	v Yorkshire	Bradford	1967

Gillete Cup – Somerset (1963-68)

BATTING:

M	Inns	NO	Runs	HS	Ave.
16	16	2	281	58*	20.07

BOWLING:

Ovs	Mdns	Runs	Wkts	Ave.	Ec. Rate
184.1	56	395	25	15.80	2.15

Man of the Match awards

v Sussex	Taunton	Rd 1	1966
v Warwickshire	Birmingham	Rd 2	1967
v Northamptonshire	Northampton	Rd 3	1967

Special Performances in League Cricket Career

1942/43   1,026 runs for Northern Districts – club record

1943/44   1,254 runs for Petersham – still a Sydney First Grade cricket record

1953   1,345 runs for Blackpool – Northern League record until 1994

INDEX

Standing the Test of Time

Standing the Test of Time